Publication design

A guide to
page layout,
typography,
format
and style

by Allen Hurlburt

Revised edition

Van Nostrand Reinhold Company

To Regina, whose patience made this book possible

Published in 1976 by Van Nostrand Reinhold Company Inc.
135 West 50th Street
New York, N.Y. 10020

Van Nostrand Reinhold Limited
1410 Birchmount Road
Scarborough, Ontario M1P 2E7, Canada

Van Nostrand Reinhold Australia Pty. Ltd.
17 Queen Street
Mitcham, Victoria 3132, Australia

Van Nostrand Reinhold Company Ltd.
Molly Millars Lane
Wokingham, Berkshire, England

16 15 14 13 12 11 10 9

Library of Congress Cataloging in Publication Data

Hurlburt, Allen, 1910-
    Publication design.

    Bibliography: p. 128
    Includes index.
    1. Magazine design. I. Title.

Z253.5.H85 1976   686.2'252   75-33846
ISBN 0-442-23592-5

Introduction to the revised edition

More than fifty years have passed since the typographic experiments of the Bauhaus designers began to set the stage for modern magazine design. Throughout those years an interaction of forces both within and outside the design profession has shaped and reshaped the form and substance of magazines. That pattern of change continues. In approaching this second edition of *Publication design* I am aware that the revolving door of shifting editors and art directors continues to turn, and familiar old titles give way to a flood of new logotypes, new formats, and new areas of specialization. This edition includes a great deal of new information and several amendments to cover the fast-moving developments of the seventies, but these have not altered the original intentions nor contradicted the validity of the original conclusions.

In preparing this edition I am indebted to the Society of Publication Designers, whose perceptive surveys of contemporary magazine design over the last ten years have provided us with a remarkably clear view of the trends and developments in publication design.

Any study of modern magazines soon reminds us that the colorful magazines that decorate the newsstands are only the visible upper portion of an iceberg. Beneath these hundred or so periodicals are several thousand business and professional publications plus countless company and institutional magazines. While many of these are low-budget publications in which visual opportunities are limited, a surprising number are impressively designed and produced. A detailed examination of these publications is beyond the scope of this book, but it is worth noting that they have influenced publishing by serving both as a training ground for art directors and as platforms for experimental design ideas.

Magazine art direction continues to be one of the most hazardous of design disciplines, but it is also in many ways one of the most rewarding. Because the magazine is essentially a personal expression of a small group, the art director can avoid the committee-dominated compromises that corrupt so much visual communication in other areas. The publication designer is also able to enjoy the increasingly rare luxury of handling a design from its inception to its final appearance on the printed page.

It is not the purpose of this book to encourage either conformity or imitation, but it is clear that the design function cannot exist in a vacuum. If the publication designer is to develop the full potential of his creative function, he will need to understand the current lines and techniques of visual communication and the basic principles that have guided other designers. In addition, he will benefit from an awareness of the forces outside the design fraternity that contribute to the success or failure of his efforts.

Contents

Introduction 3
1. The modern magazine 7
2. Elements of page design 23
3. Photographic illustration 41
4. Artwork and graphics 57
5. Format and style 67

Technical section
1. Color 82
2. The grid 87
3. Typography 91
4. Layout and production 111
   Acknowledgments 127
   Bibliography 128
   Credits 129
   Index 131

1. The modern magazine

Shifting social and scientific values, accelerated communication, and the constant compression of time and distance have probably done as much to influence the shape and form of magazines as all of the skill and talent that have gone into their creation. To meet the challenge of change, magazine designers have been forced to constantly adjust their creative approach and explore new directions in idea communication and visual presentation.

The design that we are concerned with here is a product of the twentieth century, and while its roots are in the major art upheaval that began with the postimpressionists, its measurable history does not begin until the third decade of the century.

The genesis of page design   In the early 1920s, *mise en page* — the design of the printed page — was exercising an influence on European publications. In America, a movement had begun for greater articulation and organization in the structure of magazines. The work of Heyworth Campbell in the developing art of photographic cropping and arrangement at Conde Nast, and the format styling of W. A. Dwiggins and T. M. Clelland, were making editors increasingly aware of the need for visual direction. The first issue of *Fortune,* designed by Clelland in 1930, was a milestone because it represented a magazine that unified editorial and visual concepts in its initial presentation.

Important as these developments were, magazines lacked the strong and continuous relation between art direction and editing that characterizes the modern magazine and furnishes the central focus for this study. It is not surprising that the breakthrough came under the aegis of editor Frank Crowninshield at Conde Nast. He had already placed the stamp of his rare discernment and

The 1929 *Vanity Fair* cover designed by Dr. M. F. Agha, art director, signalled the beginning of the era of the modern magazine in America.

good taste on literature and the arts when Dr. M. F. Agha joined *Vanity Fair* as art director in 1929. Thus began a remarkable period in American publishing — one that is still exercising an influence on editing and art direction. Dr. Agha was no magazine makeup artist. He entered areas of editorial judgment long denied to artists and created a magazine that brought typography, illustration, photography, and page design into a cohesion that has rarely been surpassed.

In the late twenties, shortly before Dr. Agha began shaping *Vanity Fair,* a young Parisian designer was creating some revolutionary pages for *Arts et Métiers Graphiques.* His name was Alexey Brodovitch, and he was about to cross the ocean and begin an amazing career as an advertising designer, editorial art director, and teacher.

For more than three decades, first in Philadelphia, and later in New York, he molded many eager students into exciting designers and photographers. Brodovitch became art director of *Harper's Bazaar* in 1934 and remained there

Two typical spreads from early issues of *Vanity Fair*. The one on the opposite page may well show the first bleed photograph to appear in a U.S. publication.

until 1958. Through these years, his strong influence on the advance of photography and page design continued.

The photographic revolution   During the early and mid-thirties, a lot of things happened to a lot of magazines. Some of them disappeared; among these was *Vanity Fair,* a casualty of the Depression.

An event of considerable importance in this decade was the advent of the picture magazines. The first issue of *Life* appeared on November 23, 1936, and *Look* was inaugurated two months later, in January, 1937. With their heavy emphasis on photojournalism, these two magazines attracted hosts of imitators and pulled many existing publications into their new orbit.

A book could be written about the original format of *Life,* and it would probably be classified as a "whodunit." Several typographic and design consultants, including Dr. Agha, T. M. Clelland, and Henry Dreyfus, were involved. A picture expert was brought from Ullstein, a publishing firm in Berlin. Many talented staff designers, photographers, and editors contributed their ideas to the soup that was undoubtedly stirred by the master chef, Henry Luce. The result was the rarest of events — an excellent format designed by a committee.

One of the young designers involved in the early issues of *Life* was Charles

9

Two magazine covers from the thirties. T. M. Clelland's 1930 cover for *Fortune* is in contrast to Paul Rand's 1938 approach for *Apparel Arts.*

Tudor, who was to become its art director in the early forties and guide its visual growth through nearly twenty significant years.

The changing attitude toward graphic design in the 1930s was also of importance to publishing. Several important designers from the Bauhaus in Germany arrived in America, and some young American designers were opening new areas of page design. Though they often were not publication designers, they had a broad influence on all aspects of the printed page. Three of the most important of the Americans were Lester Beall, Bradbury Thompson, and Paul Rand.

Paul Rand's layouts for *Apparel Arts* still represent a major breakthrough in the design of the printed page, and his purely graphic approach to covers set standards that have rarely been matched. Bradbury Thompson was already a skilled designer and typographer when he began his series of experiments with *Westvaco Inspirations* in 1938. Lester Beall began his impressive graphics career in Chicago, and though most of his work was in promotion and advertising, his strong designs influenced many editorial pages.

Musical chairs at the drawing board   Publishing in the first half of the forties was affected by the war. In terms of production, for example, the amount of paper magazines could use was restricted. In addition, the personnel of magazine art departments changed rapidly in a game of musical chairs that included Washington and the armed services.

Among the notable changes in this period were Charles Tudor's promotion to art director of *Life,* Dr. Agha's departure from Conde Nast, and the beginning of Alexander Liberman's long career as art director of Conde Nast Publications; he was joined by Priscilla Peck, who had worked with Brodovitch and became art editor of *Vogue.* Cipe Pineles was appointed art director of *Seventeen,* and Bradbury Thompson received the same position at *Mademoiselle.* Later, Will Burtin became art director of *Fortune* and applied his graphic approach to the scientific images that were emerging in the postwar era.

Perhaps one of the most exciting events of the 1940s was the advent of a graphic arts magazine called *Portfolio.* Conceived by Frank Zachary, its art

The first cover of *Life,* with Margaret Bourke-White's photograph, and (right) a spread from a later issue, designed by Charles Tudor.

11

Alexey Brodovitch designed the
cover for the first issue of
Portfolio as well as these spreads,
which exemplify the avante-garde
look of the magazine's pages.

director was Alexey Brodovitch. The design of its pages incorporated the best elements of the preceding revolution, and added an impressive dimension of its own. But *Portfolio* ran into the recurring problem of high-quality, high-cost magazines, and its third issue was its last.

The big picture Each decade brought new magazine art directors to the fore, and the fifties were no exception. In 1951, Frank Zachary became art director of the then three-year-old *Holiday;* his simple and direct typography and bold use of pictures gave this magazine its unique quality. In 1952, one year before I became editorial art director of *Look* and began reshaping its format, Henry Wolf came to *Esquire.* A short time later, Otto Storch joined the art staff at *McCall's,* and Arthur Paul the newly established *Playboy.*

Perhaps the single most significant event of the fifties was the introduction of *McCall's* new format in January, 1958. Its typographic inventiveness and bold page design had an immediate impact on the editorial field. It succeeded for

Portfolio ushered in the 1950s, a significant decade for magazine design, but excessive production costs ended its career after only three issues.

13

The 1954 cover for this business publication was created by Alvin Lustig.

McCall's because it was related to an editorial concept, an attempt to "rescue the American woman" from the matter-of-fact approach of most women's magazines and restore her glamour and her sense of importance. Magazines that attempted to imitate the *McCall's* style without linking design to an editorial idea soon learned that arresting design alone is not a formula for success.

A cloud passed over the magazine field during the 1950s, when one of the largest publishing firms, Crowell-Collier, decided to abandon its three important periodicals, *The American Magazine, Collier's,* and *Woman's Home Companion.* In the next decade the same fate befell the illustrious *Saturday Evening Post.* While these departures caused considerable consternation, those who knew publishing history recognized that magazines that lose touch with changing editorial requirements and reader attitudes cannot survive.

A time of change   Herb Lubalin was well known for his contributions to design in other areas when he became deeply involved with magazines in the 1960s.

Art Kane was the art director of *Seventeen* when this spread appeared in 1955. Ben Rose was the photographer.

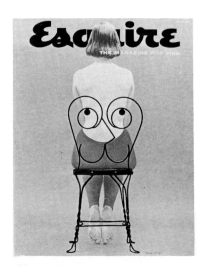

Henry Wolf designed the cover for *Esquire* in 1955 and the spread for *Harper's Bazaar* five years later.

McCall's under Otto Storch brought a new style to the women's magazines in 1959. The *Look* page (left) appeared during the same year.

Herb Lubalin designed both
Eros and *Avant Garde;* Willy
Fleckhaus was art director
of *Twen*, a German magazine.
These three magazines are
more noted for their influence
on design than their success.

Rolling Stone was one of the first magazines designed for the generation that had been brought up in front of the television screen.

His first major project was to redesign *The Saturday Evening Post.* The project failed, not because of weakness in the quality of design, but because the design was not guided by well-defined editorial concepts and consideration of the audience. Lubalin subsequently designed *Eros, Fact,* and *Avant Garde;* unfortunately, his work is noted more for its influence on page layout and typography than on the economic success of the publications.

The advent of television posed new problems for many magazines. With its effortless viewing pattern, it has become the home center for light entertainment and escape fiction. This has forced magazines to take a more serious approach in their editorial content and to concentrate on the power of words and the enduring value of the printed image.

Film documentaries and live news broadcasts, with the advantages of movement and immediacy, have dulled the once automatic appeal of photo-

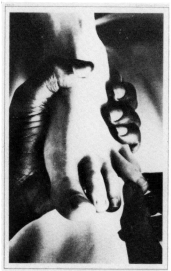

journalism. Magazines have had to adjust their visual approach to this material and concentrate on in-depth coverage.

A time of readjustment   If the fifties represented the high point of the large-format pictorial publications and the sixties represented a time of change, the seventies became the age of editorial specialization and reemphasized reader service. In October of 1971 *Look* published its last issue, and *Life* ceased publication in December, 1972. At the same time, the pressure of increasing paper costs and postal rates began to shrink the format of many continuing publications.

If the economics of the seventies placed new burdens on existing magazines, this failed to discourage the development of new publishing ventures. Scores of imitators of *Playboy* took advantage of relaxed censorship to join the "flesh" book field, and other magazines were created to cater to a multitude of special interests. In 1974 alone, nearly fifty new titles appeared on the newsstands. Though many were short-lived, a surprising number continue to seek the elusive goal of publishing success.

This 1969 cover for *Esquire* was one of the trendsetting series of concept covers designed by advertising art director George Lois and photographed by Carl Fisher.

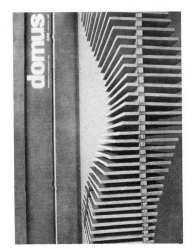

Domus, an Italian magazine devoted to architecture and design, is one of the most consistently well-designed magazines in the business and professional field.

New York brought a new style
to reader service when it
introduced features devoted
to contemporary living
and urban survival.

Playboy (above), art directed
by Arthur Paul, and *Psychology
Today* (left), under Tom Gould,
were two of the publications
that helped change the look
of magazine illustration.

The Sunday Times Magazine
was among the pioneers
in the revitalization of
the newspaper supplements.
The spreads at right
are from a feature by Will
McBride in the French
photographic magazine Zoom.

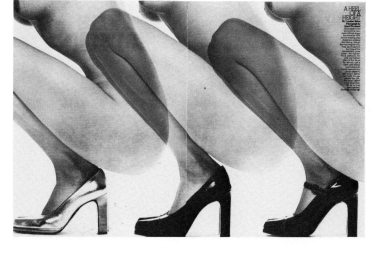

Queen (left) and *Nova* (right) were two of the London magazines that influenced the form and content of magazines in the late 1960s and early 1970s.

Perhaps the most important magazine to surface in the sixties and rise to prominence in the seventies was *New York*. It was not only regionally but demographically specialized and had a strong appeal to a young, activist urban group. Under the able editorial leadership of Clay Felker and art direction of Milton Glaser and Walter Bernard, *New York* combined advocate journalism with a new dimension in reader service dedicated to the New York life-style and the ultimate survival of its practitioners.

At the time when *New York* was developing on the East Coast, two new magazines were making their way to national recognition in California. One was *Psychology Today* and the other was *Rolling Stone*. The first was a slick, well-designed magazine addressed to the growing interest in the behavioral sciences. The other was a distant cousin of the underground newspapers associated with the hippie movement of the sixties. It began with lively coverage of rock music and the post-Dylan sound and moved on to become an impressive voice of the counterculture.

Several other magazines made significant design contributions during the seventies. *Ms.* served the women's liberation movement with a design style as independent as its subject, and magazines such as *Mineral Digest, Emergency Medicine, Back Packer,* and *Folio* (a magazine about magazines) demon-

21

strated the importance of good design in highly specialized publications.

American magazine design of the twenties and thirties developed under the influence of the graphic design revolution in Europe. This process was reversed in the postwar years when the success of the popular large-circulation magazines in America began to affect the shape and style of publications in Britain and on the Continent. By the 1970s these magazines developed a new vitality of their own, and American designers found themselves again turning to Europe and Britain for some of their ideas and inspiration. The work of Willy Fleckhaus on *Twen* in Germany, the French magazine *Zoom,* and the new magazines and the redesigned supplements of the London Sunday and weekend newspapers all played significant roles in this shift of influence.

Back in the early thirties the bleed photograph broke the conventional borders and margins of the past. For nearly four decades pictures bleeding off the edges of the page were the hallmark of the modern magazine, but as picture cropping became tighter and pages became more and more crowded, designers began reaching back to the white margin and occasional ornamental borders for contrast and change of pace.

In the sixties magazine illustration began to move away from straightforward realism and fall under the influence of surrealism and the decorative arts. In typography letter-spacing and wide leading were once considered proof that a magazine was modern, but today tight spacing and minimum leading are the fashionable solution. These gyrations of taste continue, but beyond the reach of fads and fancies, certain guiding principles of design and presentation developed over half a century continue to influence the form of successful magazine pages. It is with these basic foundations of good design that this book is concerned.

2. Elements of page design

As in other areas of design, the merely pleasing arrangement of elements is rarely an adequate solution to the problem of page layout. Only when the design becomes a visual and typographic synthesis of the basic editorial idea projected in dynamic form can it be considered a true solution.

Because the success of every layout is finally measured by the way in which it serves the editorial objective, the designer cannot detach himself from the process of communication and the personal level at which it finally takes place. No matter how large or small a magazine's audience is, no matter how it is distributed, or how often each copy changes hands, that audience is made up of individuals, and the significant exchange takes place only when each individual reader picks up his copy and opens its pages.

When the printed page was designed for the book, ease of reading and quiet consistency of format was the primary requisite. The work of Gutenberg and the printers of Mainz, with its heavy medieval letter forms, seemed to defy easy reading, but when the center of printing was transferred to the scholar-printers of Italy at the end of the fifteenth century, the page took on an impressive Renaissance beauty and clarity.

The volume that did the most to shape the typographic form of books was the *Poliphilus (Hypnertomachi Poliphili),* printed in 1499 in Venice by Aldus Manutius with a roman letter cut by Francesco Griffo. The beauty of the letter form, its setting and page proportion still stand as a model for contemporary book design after nearly five centuries.

While it is helpful for the contemporary publication designer to study the classic models, his problem is light-years removed from that of the book designer. Today, we are exposed to a virtual barrage of visual impressions. Projected and printed images pass before our eyes until most of them become blurred and meaningless. The designer's role is to bring his pages out of this clutter and confusion and, at the same time, break through the wall of apathy surrounding the modern reader.

Page design is a complex combination of many forces — the designer's taste and talent, his knowledge, and his experience, balanced against the content and the editorial concept to be projected. Because this process is often intuitive and creative, it defies scientific analysis and formulas. Yet, it can be helpful to study the principles of design, if only to form a frame of reference. Conventional boundaries can be broken only when we know what they are.

Any study of page design is best begun with an awareness of the space

These early pages from the *Poliphilus,* designed at the close of the fifteenth century, still stand as models for book design but are far removed from modern magazine needs.

produceffe,quali fono quefti nel diuo fronte affixi, di quefto **cælico** fig mento præfulgidi &amorofi,Et percio per tanti iurgii obfeffo el trifto co re & da tanta difcrepante controuerfia de appetifcentia fuftiniua , Quale fi tra effi una fronde del aftante lauro del tumulo del R e de Bibria in me dio collocata fuffe, Ne unque la rixa ceffare,fi non reiecta, Et cufi penfita ua non ceffabondo tanto litigio,fi non da effo core tanto piacere de coftei (non factibile)fuffe ablato. Et per tale ragione non fe potea firmaméte có uenire el uoluptico & inexplebile defio de luno ne de laltro, Quale homo da fame exarcebato & tra multiplici & uarii eduli fremente, de tutti cupi do di niuno integramente rimane di lardente appetito contento , Ma de Bulimia in fecto.

LA BELLISSIMA NYMPHA AD POLIPHILO PER-
VENTA, CVM VNA FACOLA NELLA SINISTRA MA
NV GERVLA, ET CVM LA SOLVTA PRESOLO, LOIN
VITA CVM ESSA ANDARE, ET QVIVI POLIPHI-
LO INCOMINCIA PIV DA DOLCE AMORE
DELLA ELEGANTE DAMIGEL
LA CONCALEFACTO, GLI
SENTIMENTI INFLAM
MARSENE.

ESPECTANDO PRAESENTIALMENTE EL reale & intelligibile obiecto duna præftantiffima repræ fentatione de tanta uenuftiffima præfentia & diuo afpe cto, & de uno copiofo aceruo & uniuerfale aggregatione de inuifa bellecia & inhumana formofitate, Exiguo & exile per quefto & impare reputaua tutte anteuidute iex-

24

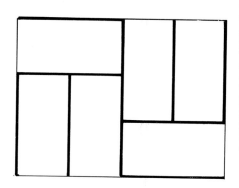

The Japanese sense of asymmetrical order anticipated modern design by several centuries. The tatami mat's double-square proportion functions as a major module of Japanese architecture.

in which the action takes place. This area is of necessity a carefully prescribed rectangle with certain traditional boundaries. The size of the rectangle varies from the pocket-size publications to the full display sizes of the highly visual general magazines, and the dimensions are more often dictated by economics and mechanical limitations than by aesthetic considerations.

The dynamics of space   One of the earliest and simplest systems of organizing space was the tatami mat. This module, approximately three feet by six feet, set the pattern for the serenely beautiful, traditional architecture of Japan. Based on the double square, the mats were laid vertically and horizontally in a carefully conceived pattern. Some of the resulting space designs bear a marked, if coincidental, relation to the later works of Mondrian and other artists and architects of the de Stijl movement, which had a dominating influence on design in Europe from 1912 to 1920.

25

In the development of modern design, the de Stijl movement is credited with the synthesis of cubism into ordered form. The illustrations above show van Doesburg's formula for two-dimensional design and one of Mondrian's unique solutions to the division of space.

De Stijl was born of the cubist revolution in painting, which is generally conceded to be the foundation of modern design. Theo van Doesburg and Piet Mondrian, the leading painters of de Stijl, showed that the dynamic division of space could become an aesthetic experience and that rhythm, tension, and order could be drawn from the asymmetrical approach to form. Both these artists were remarkably expressive in their design attitudes, Mondrian in his neoplasticist manifesto and van Doesburg in his perhaps oversimplified formulas of space utilization.

One of the designers who expanded the innovations of de Stijl was Le Corbusier. Himself a product of the cubist movement, his architecture, design, and paintings may have had a greater impact on modern design than any individual in this century. He developed an elaborate module for the division of space based on the measurement of man. To offset the symmetry of the human figure, he raised the left arm, and based his modular theory on three main points: the solar plexus, the top of the head, and the tip of the extended fingers. These points yielded a mean and an extreme ratio (golden mean), which Le Corbusier translated into an infinite series of proportions. Perhaps this complex modular system is of more value to architecture than page design, but it demonstrates an interesting system that develops an asymmetrical design out of a symmetrical mean.

In addition to his superb use of asymmetrical balance, Le Corbusier's designs reveal the important principle of developing volume from within an area. His sketch for the "Growing Museum" is an example of this important principle at work: the form spirals outward from a carefully selected point of origin.

The grid system has many champions among contemporary graphic designers. When it is used with sensitivity and imagination, it can produce handsome, well-ordered magazine units. When it is applied to all elements of a format, it can also generate a sense of continuity and flow that has a distinctive unifying value. When it is used without sufficient skill, it can become a straitjacket that produces dull layouts and a rigid format.

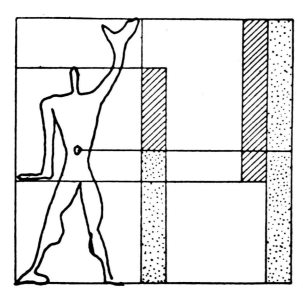

Le Corbusier developed an elaborate modular system for space design based on the human proportions, which he then extended to a series of mathematically developed golden sections.

Though artists and designers have used grids of one kind or another for centuries to assist in composition, proportionate enlargement, and perspective drawing, its application to modern page design is a relatively recent development of Swiss designers and teachers.

I have generally opposed the grid system in my own work because I find it inhibiting to the dramatic changes in form that add surprise and excitement to visual presentation. While I have avoided the formality of a tightly prestructured system, however, through the years I have developed a sense of order (an imaginary grid system) that I have applied consciously or subconsciously to the division of space within my designs.

A major virtue of the grid system is the discipline it imposes on the untrained designer. I favor a free approach to design problems, even if it entails the violation of what seem like rules or formulas. There are no ''don'ts'' that cannot be abridged, nor any design laws that are absolute. However, a designer should understand the nature of order and have some awareness of the framework from which he is departing. For these reasons a more detailed explanation of the grid system is included in the technical section of this book.

The balance in modern layouts is more like that of a tightrope walker and her parasol than that of a seesaw or measuring scales. A tightrope walker in continuous and perfect balance is not much more interesting than someone walking on a concrete sidewalk. It is only through threatened imbalance, tension, and movement that the performance achieves interest and excitement.

Le Corbusier's study of space relationships also suggested that design can begin within a space and then develop outward, as in his plan for the expanding museum.

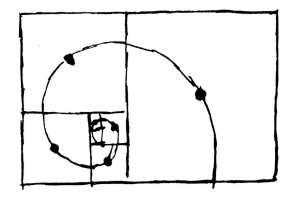

Architecturally and professionally, there's only one way to go

ONE WAY

For the men who make it new, turn page

One of the simplest of graphic symbols—the one-way sign— takes on a new meaning and adds graphic surprise to the design when it is pointed upward.

New natural look

in sun and water

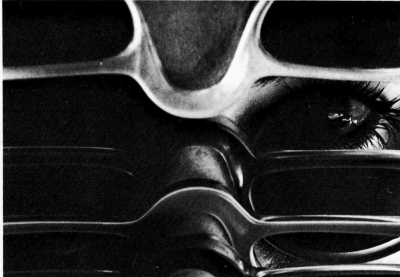

MANY WOMEN feel that the greatest beauty treatment in the world is a good tan. Americans especially worship the sun. But they are learning that the natural, even the freckled look (above, left), is preferable to the deep tan that hardens, eventually ruins the skin. Beauties like star Samantha Eggar and the model pictured here are really showing their freckles this year. Others are painting them on with eyebrow pencil. Another swing back to nature that most males will welcome is fewer false eyelashes. Besides, they come off underwater. A good waterproof mascara is what a woman needs when she shakes the liquid aquamarines out of her eyes and gazes straight and smiling into a man's.

For flirting on the beach, there are delightful demi-sunglasses in a rainbow range of lens tints and frame colors as shown above. They don't interfere with the communication from a beautiful pair of eyes.

The ideal sunbath is one tempered with an occasional plunge. Swimming is good for the figure, and it will keep the hot winter-resort sun from frying the skin. The suntan of the future has a golden tone, has to be nursed as gently as a vacation romance.

Freckles are in, deep tans are out

62 LOOK 5/7/68   PHOTOGRAPHED BY MAX MAXWELL   continued

This spread design develops outward as the Le Corbusier snail design suggests and it also bears a marked relationship to Van Doesburg's theories of space organization.

For the modern magazine designer and the tightrope walker, balance is a matter of feeling rather than formula.

Paul Rand, in his excellent book *Thoughts on Design,* states it this way, "Exact symmetry offers the spectator too simple and too obvious a statement. It offers him little or no intellectual pleasure, no challenge. For the pleasure derived from observing asymmetric arrangements lies partly in overcoming resistance which, consciously or not, the spectator adjusts in his own mind, thus acquiring some sort of aesthetic satisfaction."

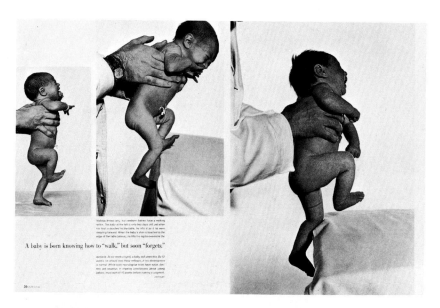

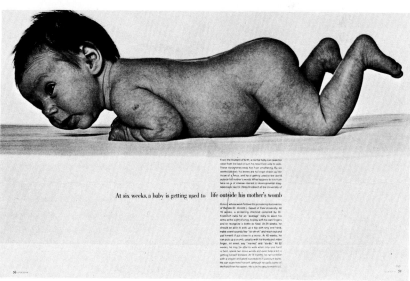

These pages suggest how vertical and horizontal forms can alter the static effect of a constant rectangle.

The contrast of size and value
and the successful handling of
tone variation by photographer
Bert Stern gives this layout
its quality and strength.

Value relationship If the Japanese were among the first to study the asymmetrical and ordered division of space, they were also among the first to explore value relationships in their traditional *sumi* painting and their precise architecture. They used the word *notan* to decribe the delicate yet often forceful balance of the gradations of dark and light.

The white of the paper and the strongest black that the printing press can achieve are the polar forces in the design process. Because we are also concerned with all of the steps between black and white, value is a complex and

As frail as a butterfly and as fast as the wind, the debonair little *Antoinette* could carry her master close to the sun and the stars, to dizzy heights where the eagle soared. Some pioneer airmen learned that answers to this celestial sightseeing weren't always to be found in "the book." New chapters had to be continually written—often the bumpiest way. Above, a literal-minded German pilot struggles to fly by the numbers.

continued

46 LOOK 11-5-68

Carefully cropped photographs enhance the continuity of the series of photographs at the left and contrast in image size adds to the overall effect.

important ingredient in page layout. The study of value applies to color images as well as those in black and white; color pictures can be studied for their qualities of lightness and darkness completely apart from their variations in chromatic value.

In contemporary design, the distribution of the values within a photograph or drawn illustration often determines the quality of its composition, and the interrelationship of the tones in groups of these photographs or drawings can dictate their arrangement in the finished design.

33

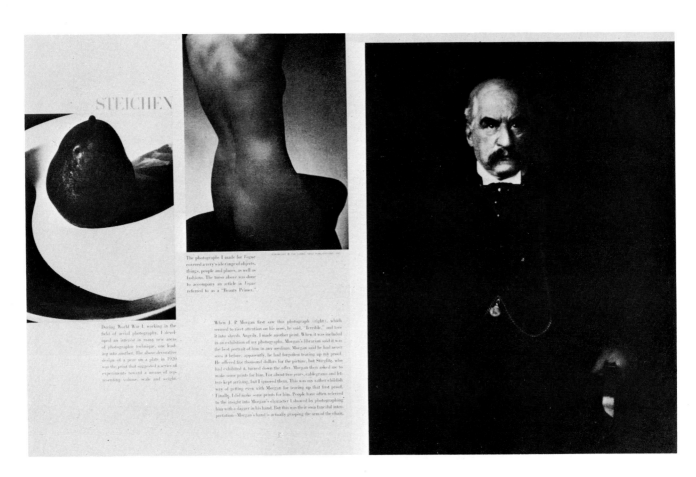

The photographs I made for *Vogue* covered a very wide range of objects, things, people and places, as well as fashions. The torso above was done to accompany an article in *Vogue* referred to as a "Beauty Primer."

During World War I, working in the field of aerial photography, I developed an interest in many new areas of photographic technique, one leading into another. The above decorative design of a pear on a plate in 1920 was the print that suggested a series of experiments toward a means of representing volume, scale and weight.

When J. P. Morgan first saw this photograph (right), which seemed to rivet attention on his nose, he said, "Terrible," and tore it into shreds. Angrily, I made another print. When it was included in an exhibition of my photographs, Morgan's librarian said it was the best portrait of him in any medium. Morgan said he had never seen it before; apparently, he had forgotten tearing up my proof. He offered five thousand dollars for the picture, but Stieglitz, who had exhibited it, turned down the offer. Morgan then asked me to make some prints for him. For about two years, cablegrams and letters kept arriving, but I ignored them. This was my rather childish way of getting even with Morgan for tearing up that first proof. Finally, I did make some prints for him. People have often referred to the insight into Morgan's character I showed by photographing him with a dagger in his hand. But this was their own fanciful interpretation—Morgan's hand is actually grasping the arm of the chair.

The intrigue of color should not blind us to the power and beauty of black-and-white images. In these classic Edward Steichen photographs, the composition and the value relationships create their own visual excitement.

Contrast   The study of value leads naturally to an awareness of the possibilities of contrast as a design force. When a dark image (low key) is positioned adjacent to a light image (high key), the resulting contrast often enhances both images and adds visual impact to the layout. Because, in nature, the nearer an object, is, the darker it seems, the use of dark and light contrast can also enhance the dimensional illusion.

The principles of contrast can be applied to color images; for example, muted tones play against colors of high saturation, and cool colors oppose

The deliberately cropped image of the boy and man seems even larger in contrast with the smaller photographs. The dark silhouette and the high key photograph are enhanced by value contrast.

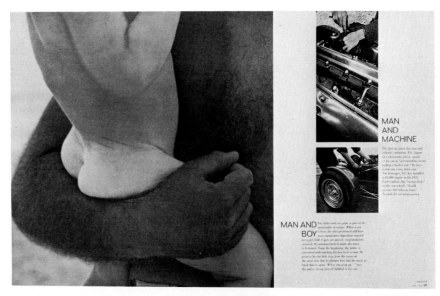

An ocean of wheat and a sea of cars seeming to stretch beyond the curvature of the earth signify   prosperity, employment and industrial evolution in the Midwest

Big combines harvest bumper wheat crop near Kenneth, Kan.

Cars of workers pack parking area at Boeing's Wichita plant

In this spread a special camera creates a planned distortion to make these two photographs work as though they were one.

warm colors. Chromatic contrast — the juxtaposition of complementary or discordant colors — can also be a positive force in page design.

Another form of contrast worth noting is the contrast of volume. A large picture often seems to be even larger in the presence of a small one, and extreme size variations can make the total design space seem larger than it actually is. The effect of volume contrast may seem obvious, but it is my impression that more dull and uninteresting layouts are guilty of uniformity of scale, than any other fault.

36

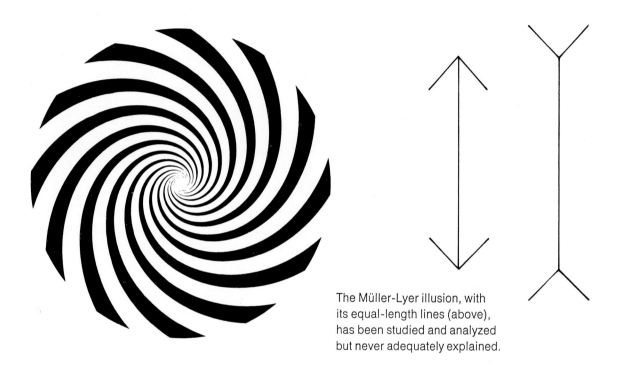

The Müller-Lyer illusion, with
its equal-length lines (above),
has been studied and analyzed
but never adequately explained.

In this common optical illusion
the spiral seems to shrink
and then expand as it turns,
though its size is constant.

The contrast of form — exaggeration of the horizontal or vertical dimension
of an image — can also affect our perception of space. Strong vertical emphasis
can make a space seem taller than it is, and horizontal emphasis can make it
seem wider.

Perception and illusion   The preceding paragraphs have taken for granted
the importance of illusion as a design force: our perception of depth, size, and
shape depends on variable factors.

In their exploration of the phenomena of perception, the Gestalt psychologists learned that the mind tends to organize sensory data into combinations
that form objects. This permits us to see images that aren't really there, such as
the man in the moon, or castles in the clouds. It also permits us to put pieces

37

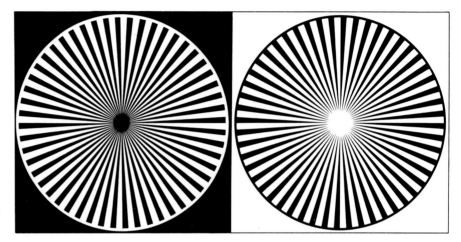

The retinal response stimulated by this composition called *Cinematic Painting* by Ludwig suggests not only vibration but even color that isn't there.

of a puzzle together before we have picked them up and, on the printed page, to accept the illusion of halftone dots, understand the simplified form of a cartoon, or find meaning in an abstraction. It also assists the eye in accepting perspective — the illusion of three dimensions on the two-dimensional surface.

This phenomenon of vision, the ability of eye and mind to assemble and arrange elements, is at the root of the design process and is the key to effective design. All the visual forces we have dealt with are affected by the Gestalt concept, and it is in this difficult-to-define area that others will see and judge the results of our work. The fact that what the eye perceives is not necessarily what the designer intended should not be overlooked.

When viewers group objects and come up with a perceptual hypothesis that is incorrect, the result is an illusion: we invert perspective, misjudge scale and value, and sometimes see objects and colors that do not exist in the area we are viewing.

There are many examples of illusion — one is the Müller-Lyer illusion in which lines of equal length seem shorter or longer when direct or inverted arrow heads are applied to the ends; other illusions are the spiral that moves inward or outward, the line that appears bent when other lines are juxtaposed to it. When we look at an aerial view of a mountainous landscape with the shadows cast to our right, or to the bottom of the picture, we read it without difficulty, but if we turn it upside down, the shadows falling upward, what seemed like

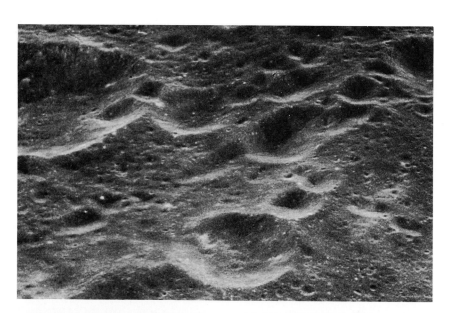

When the light source in the lunar photograph (top) comes from above, the eye sees the craters as concave shapes, but when the picture is turned and the light comes from below, they look more like hills.

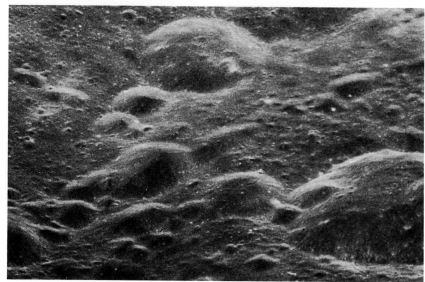

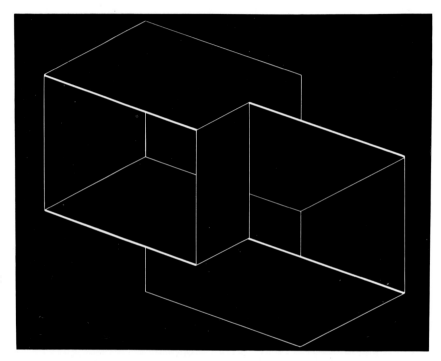

Josef Albers created this perspective paradox in his book *Despite Straight Lines.* He describes our confusion in seeing 'the cubes at right from below, at left from above.''

mountains before may now look like valleys. One only needs to spend a little time with optical art to witness these illusions in their most dramatic manifestations.

The study of perception is a fascinating but not essential exploration for the designer. In general, he should use illusion sparingly, not so much to fool the eye as to aid it in responding to an image and understanding an idea.

The preceding paragraphs bring together some of the principles that guide modern page design. It would be a mistake to consider these as evidence that design is a scientific process. Design is a creative and intuitive action that brings editorial ideas into focus with reader involvement. Many of the most successful designs for the printed page violate all rules of order and logic. In spite of this, the skilled designer is usually familiar with the principles guiding page design and aware of the pitfalls that lurk in the path of contrived and self-indulgent results.

40

3. Photographic illustration

Though there are magazines that are best designed with words alone, and others that may find a successful framework exclusively in photographs or in drawn illustrations, most publication designers rely on all three for their visual presentation.

In the early days of periodical publishing, decisions on illustrations were determined by physical considerations. When type and crude woodcuts were the only printing materials available, words were of primary importance. Later, steel engravings were used to translate the artist's work into a rough equivalent in printed form. Finally, the halftone dot brought freedom of selection to editors.

Even after the advent of the halftone, the primary visual treatment was drawn illustration. Photographs were used rarely, and then only for factual documentation. Gradually, as the nature of magazines changed, and camera and reproduction techniques improved, the photograph began to assume a more important role.

This great reservoir of content received little attention from publishing until the emergence of the picture magazines in the 1930s. The impact of photo-journalism was staggering. Not only were the picture magazines immediate successes, but their influence began to change the face of existing publications. The revolution extended to almost every form of visual presentation — advertising, books, newspapers, and direct mail.

Photography does not fall easily into categories, but the use of photographs in communication can be broken down into definable areas. A description of these areas will serve as a guide to understanding the role of photography in the modern magazine.

Coverage of the Oklahoma dust bowl and Birmingham show how photojournalism in expert hands can convert a merely newsworthy moment into an enduring visual document.

Photojournalism　This is a broad term that is sometimes used to cover all magazine photography, but it most commonly applies to the ability of the camera to see and report the events in the life of man.

The picture story　Though there is such a thing as a single storytelling picture, the term *picture story* usually applies to a group of pictures. Picture stories usually follow the pattern of prose stories and, like their literary counter-

43

The story of a President and his son

LAURA BERGQUIST
in Look, December 3, 1963

HE'S JUST THREE YEARS OLD, and sturdy, brown-eyed John Fitzgerald Kennedy, Jr., obviously finds life in the White House just marvelous. Not that he's aware of what his father does for a living, or why he gets lifts in helicopters so regularly. Like many a two-year-old, John John was a late talker. Then, in Hyannis Port this summer, he bloomed—words and ideas bubble out of this small boy, loud and fast. Off and on, John John dashes into the Presidential office with late bulletins from the playground. The President called him John John almost from the day he was born, to avoid well-worn nicknames like Jack or Johnny. Anything that flies intrigues JFK, Jr.—planes, rockets, blimps and, oh boy, helicopters, which only six months ago he pronounced "hopycops." Daddy, who always seems to be flying someplace, is good about bringing home surprises: like a life-sized toy parrot, with a mysterious tape recorder inside. Press a button, and a fatherly voice you know says with a Boston twang, "My name is Poll Parrot. Would you like to come fly with me in my helicopter?" "Hi there, Poll Parrot," answers John John with aplomb. "Would you like a stick of gum?"

The helicopter from Washington that's whirling down to a landing on the pad means that Daddy's back, and what loyal son and greeter would ever want to miss a homecoming?

Sometimes, when you dash in to see your father, he's talking to a bunch of strange people and firmly nudges you out of his office. Just before bed is usually the best time for good talk and play.

The picture story is at its best when it focuses on a single individual in terms of a universal experience. Stanley Tretick's camera tells such a story here and on the following three pages.

parts, they require the familiar introduction, body, and conclusion. At their best, picture stories have a simple single focus, preferably an individual. They frequently tell about experiences common to many people by focusing on one. Many pictures must be shot to get one that can be used.

The picture essay   In the picture essay, related pictures are used to convey editorial ideas about a place or a situation. In general, the essay is broader in focus than the picture story. The terms are used rather loosely in photo-

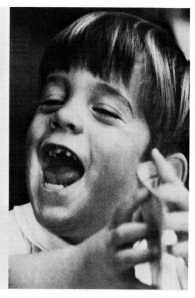

We're playing right outside Daddy's airplane. It's James, the patrol talks. He's with Daddy's niece. It's been a grand week for punches from all kinds of people who came to see Daddy. Someone just named Mr. Aslaska dropped by from a place called the Congo, and felt a named Alaska dude, just John John says.

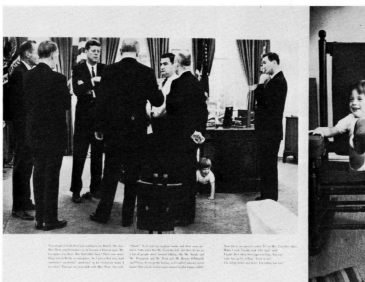

You can easily find just waiting to see Daddy. Oh-don Miss Shaw and Grandma go in because a Baroness was, Mr. Estinghin was there. Was that office that? There was something feel in Berlin or someplace. So I just yelled very loud "surprise! surprise! surprise!" so he suddenly knew I was there. That got me in trouble with Miss Shaw. She said, "Shush." So I told my airplane banks and then come go there. Later when Mr. Grandm feld, and they let me in. A lot of people stood around talking, like Mr. Bundy and Mr. Thompson and Mr. Bush and Mr. Kenny O'Donnell and Pierre. It was pretty boring, so I crawled into my secret house, but nobody in that room wanted to play bunny rabbit. Now this is my special rocker. It's in Mrs. Lincoln's office. When I rock I really rock with rigor, until I make Miss Shaw feel just watching. You can make her up by telling "Look it out, I'm riding faster and faster. I'm riding too fast!"

A boy's practically best friend is Mrs. Evelyn Lincoln, the President's secretary. She'll always laugh at your jokes, and she has a big, big supply of pens and crayons for drawing, while you wait to see father. The most fun place to play is under Daddy's desk. It's got lots more space there than you'd think. You see, the idea is to close it and hide. Then you get everybody around to search and ask, "Is the canny rabbit in there?" When you don't see, then go invisible, surprised. About 5:45 p.m. is a good time to call on Daddy. Nearly everybody's gone home, and you can wear pants and funny little felt shoes and no socks. I don't mind if you play myself under the desk. I call that plain "hot house," even thought you didn't Caroline found the secret door first. During the day, I'd prefer have myself. My sister Miss Shaw and I go to special trips by the door. I have to look at the window.

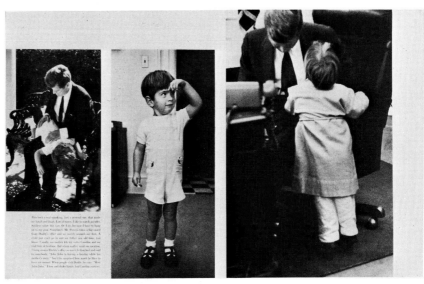

This isn't a real spanking, just a pretend one, that made us laugh and laugh. Lots of times, I like to watch parades. Soldiers salute like Gov. Or I do, because I have to hang on to my gun. Sometimes Mr. Powers takes a big camel from Daddy's office and we snitch snouts out first. A child just can't go to visit my father any old time, not know. Usually, we mothers let my sister Caroline and me visit him at birthday. But when mother went on vacation, I bring over Davis's office so much for laughed and said to somebody, "John John is having a birthday while his mother's away." You'd be surprised how much he likes to have me around. When people visit Daddy, he says, "Meet John John." I bow and shake hands. Isn't mothee curious.

46

PHOTOGRAPHED BY ERNST HAAS

STONEHENGE
"HUGE FRAME OF GIANT HANDS,
THE MIGHTY PILE . . .
VICTORY'S IDOL VAST,
AN UNHEWN SHRINE."
Thomas Warton

SPRING Englishmen treasure their spring. "It warms the world anew," said Algernon Charles Swinburne. James Thomson wrote, "Fair-handed Spring unbosoms every grace," and Robert Browning longed to be in England "now that April's there." Winter is a long, dark, marrow-chilling experience for the English. But **COMES** in February, crocuses begin to bloom in the **TO ENGLAND** Scilly Isles. The season marches slowly north, through Cornwall, past Salisbury Plain (above), past London and into the Midlands. Now, once again, the land shakes itself alive. Spring, in the words of Shakespeare, "hath put a spirit of youth in everything."

THE CATHEDRAL AT ELY
"SPRING HANGS
HER INFANT BLOSSOMS
ON THE TREES,
ROCK'D IN THE CRADLE
OF THE WESTERN BREEZE."
William Cowper

The photo essay has a broader focus than the picture story. This opening spread from an essay by Ernst Haas deals with time and place. The design is by Verne Noll.

journalism, and what one magazine may call a story, another may describe as an essay.

Photographic illustration   Here the camera is used to illustrate an already-formed editorial idea or an existing object. This category includes the illustration of fiction and nonfiction, as well as copy on fashion, food, and architecture.

The collaboration of art director and photographer is important in many areas

John Vachon achieves a documentary quality in his profile of the Great Plains. Joe Tarallo was the designer.

The photo essay form can apply to general subject areas. These pages are samples of an essay called "The Songs of Freedom" by Art Kane.

of magazine design. In the case of stories shot in the field, it may merely involve the designer's translation of the photographer's intention, but in photographic illustrations, it often becomes more direct.

There are times when the photographer and art director may work together in the studio and design the page on the ground glass of the camera. There are other times when a photographer must follow a preconceived layout in composing his pictures. The precise method of operation in these circumstances depends on the individual art director and photographer.

50

We shall overcome.

We shall overcome,
We shall overcome someday.
Oh, deep in my heart,
I do believe
We shall overcome someday.

When the art director is overspecific in his direction of the photographic assignment, he may inhibit the creative freedom of the photographer and limit his contribution. On the other hand, if his results are to coincide with editorial intentions, the photographer needs to know as much as possible about these intentions and about the conditions under which the picture will be used.

Photographic technique　In recent years, considerable emphasis has been placed on technique as a creative factor in photography. The textural effect of

51

This portrait of Picasso is enhanced by its background of Vauvenargues and the arc of a fortuitous rainbow.

Humor, a too infrequent quality in photography, comes through in Richard Avedon's composite portrait. Design by Philip Sykes

The low camera angle and the short focus lens add to the sense of movement in this documentary photograph.

enlarged grain or reticulation, the blur of motion or diffusion, and the calculated distortion of special lenses, filters, or cameras can all enhance the photographic effect when used with purpose and skill, but there is growing evidence that a preoccupation with technique often smothers the important pictorial purpose of photography.

Picture selection　Though some preliminary screening of pictures is done by photographers, editors, or picture departments, the art director must examine thousands of pictures in the course of a year. Selections resulting in as few as a dozen published pictures sometimes must be made from as many as three thousand original exposures.

　The difficulty of selecting pictures is increased by the current saturation of visual impressions, which swiftly reduce yesterday's brilliant ideas to tomorrow's tired cliches. This means that we cannot afford to be rigid in our standards or even completely logical in our search for pictures. The primary ingredients of picture success in a magazine are surprise and impact. This does not mean that a picture need always be shocking or sensational. Often a quiet

On these two pages are a few of the many technical possibilities in photography. By sandwiching two identical transparencies, Art Kane creates a startling view of San Marco.

picture can be both surprising and powerful. Nor does it mean that we can ignore logic in the process of picture selection. There are certain factors that have a distinct bearing on the success of the search:

1. First consideration goes to the appropriateness of the photograph in relation to the editorial message. We have a responsibility to the editorial idea and the direct communication of that idea to the reader.

2. The second consideration is the believability or truthfulness of a picture. Does it have a stilted or contrived look? Sometimes a completely honest

54

Philippe Halsman combined two exposures on the same film to create a Janus-like image of Huntley and Brinkley (above), and Marvin Newman used a zoom exposure (right) to add dimension to sports action.

photograph can look false, so we must be concerned with effect more than with the evidence.

3. Only after the first two considerations have been satisfied can we turn to the design values: composition, tonal treatment, and surface quality. Though the needs of content must be met, it is at this third step that the dynamic concept of presentation enters the process.

4. Because picture layouts rarely consist of single pictures, finally we must consider the relation of photographs to each other and to the structure of the completed story.

This list implies that the various considerations are a series of steps to be taken one at a time. In reality they work as a single conditioned reaction as the designer narrows the choice from hundreds of pictures to the final few the layout requires.

Picture selection and picture layout are often part of the same process. As the designer reviews photographs, he is organizing the spaces they will eventually occupy and assigning the images to their place in a total structure.

An experienced designer can sometimes scan a group of pictures and

55

Modern science has created new sources for photographic drama. Neil Armstrong used an automated camera for his historic Apollo 11 picture.

simultaneously construct a multiple page layout in his mind's eye. Usually, the solutions are not this simple. He will have to amend and adapt his design as he sketches his layouts and works out the details of cropping, positioning, and relating the photographs to typographic matter.

Whether the solution comes easily or only after a struggle, it is the mark of a good designer to be critical of his own solutions. He will know when to polish his ideas further and when not to ''noodle'' a good idea to death. For most designers this analysis will be most successful when some time elapses between conceiving the layout and reappraising it. Sometimes a layout will be discarded at this point for a new and occasionally totally different solution. Sometimes no matter how many fresh approaches are attempted, the original conception cannot be improved.

56

4. Artwork and graphics

American illustration was born in the painterly tradition of Eakins, Homer, and Bingham, at the end of the nineteenth century. It was pioneered in the early twentieth century by illustrators such as N. C. Wyeth, J. C. Leyendecker, Norman Rockwell, Maxfield Parrish, and Wallace Morgan. But its golden era came in the thirties and forties, when superb draftsmen like Robert Fawcett and Austin Briggs, dramatic illustrators like Harold Von Schmidt and Peter Helk, and romantic illustrators like Al Parker and John La Gatta joined the painters, and brought their impressive talents to magazine pages. This was the era of great fiction when *The Saturday Evening Post, Colliers,* and a different kind of *Cosmopolitan* flourished. As television became the primary medium of escape, causing the decline of fiction as a major attraction in magazines, and as the photographic revolution swept away some of the need for drawn images, this period came to an end, but this was not the end of illustration.

Some illustrators began to adapt themselves to the new informational needs of magazines, and a new breed of illustrators began to challenge the camera with imaginative, sometimes decorative, styles, and a general break with the representational approach to drawn images.

The Push Pin Studio and its assembled group of talented, often intellectual, artists were in the vanguard of this movement. A preoccupation with "camp" images by gallery artists such as Andy Warhol, Roy Lichtenstein, and Robert Rauschenberg began to exercise its own influence on a more varied, less purely representational approach to illustration. One other force that helped to turn the style of drawn illustration away from old images was a growing

A profile of the city created for LOOK by **Ben Shahn**

Instead of the traditional photographic opening, this special issue of *Look* began with the surprise of a new Ben Shahn drawing.

interest in science and the abstract, or graphic, imagery that works with this kind of editorial content.

There is no simple dividing line between the areas appropriate to photography and those best served by drawn illustration. A photograph can occasionally serve fiction with a new kind of power. In news documentation a drawing can re-create the mood of a moment that was not available to the camera. In some instances, a graphic design can convey more information than any number of photographs or drawings.

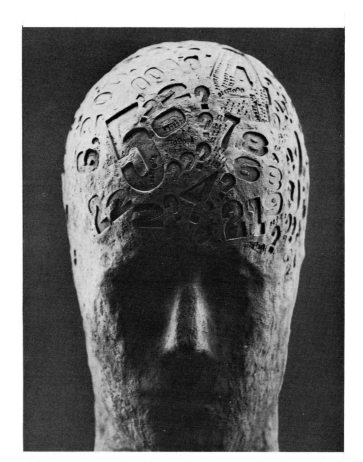

These are two examples of the use of combined media in contemporary illustration. Both Jack Gregory's sculpture and Paul Davis's painted object need photography to be complete.

The following editorial classifications are often, but not always, best covered by drawn illustration:

Fiction   The old and still excellent form of narrative illustration created situations that made the reader want to know the outcome and compelled him to read the text. Those situations can be made believable in illustration, but they usually seem contrived and false in photography.

Humor   The cartoon has been a mainstay of many magazines, and it is rarely challenged by the camera.

59

These two illustrations were photographic impossibilities. The one by Robert Fawcett is of a bit of nonexistent history, and the one by Austin Briggs re-creates an event that had no photographic record.

History   The obvious inadequacy and unavailability of existing photographic illustration makes this an important area for the artist and illustrator.

Science   Illustration and graphics are playing an important role in clarifying the fast developments of modern science. The challenge of creating appropriate illustrations will grow as we move toward multidimensional concepts and a new perception of reality.

World and national affairs   When we find ourselves using tired photographs

from the wire services to illustrate serious features, a search for graphic solutions is indicated.

Charts, maps, pictograms, tables, and graphs are areas that magazine designers frequently neglect. In the current information explosion, these materials serve as valuable communications tools. Because they are sometimes complex combinations of typographic and illustrative elements, they pose problems that are difficult to solve, but the solutions need not be dull.

The designer's success in using photography, artwork, or graphics is

For over fifty years Norman
Rockwell's paintings have been
part of America. Here he
delineates three aspects of the
contemporary scene. Two of the
originals are large oils; in
one he shows his versatility
with a rare, Goyaesque sketch.

Humor comes more naturally
to drawing than to photography,
as these drawings by André
François and David Levine
effectively demonstrate.

influenced by the financial resources of the publication, but a low budget does
not justify a poor job. It is the designer's role to find within his limitations an
imaginative solution that is effective without being costly. By using new, under-
exposed talent, and by creating a showcase for the work of established artists
and photographers through a handsome format, the designer can often
overcome the limitations of his budget.

It is important that the art director supply artists, as well as photographers,

Three illustrations for a
series of articles show a variety
of visual ideas. Milton Glaser
used collage for Adam Smith;
George Giusti, bold color for
Caesar; and for Jefferson
Look used a cropped closeup
of Rembrandt Peale's portrait.

Bernie Fuchs's boldly composed portraits were used here instead of the all-too-familiar photographs.

with as much information as possible, but it is equally important that he not place them in the straitjacket of a preconceived form, a tightly rendered layout. Some artists will accept, and often require, more direction than others, but in most cases when a comprehensive sketch is required in advance of the finished art work, the artist should be given the opportunity to make his own sketch. The concept of an illustration is a shared responsibility, but usually the finished result is the primary responsibility of the artist or photographer.

5. Format and style

A magazine is much more than single well-designed units strung together. The magazine designer must concern himself with the continuity of page to page and spread to spread through the total magazine, and finally he must relate his designs from issue to issue to project the personality of the publication.

The character of a magazine is determined by its editorial objectives and its approach to communication, but its style is drawn from these elements plus the form of its presentation.

Style is difficult to define and not easily arrived at. Even the most skillfully designed format usually does not correctly reflect the personality of a publication until many issues and sometimes many seasons pass. But it is in the successful achievement of this unity that a designer succeeds or fails.

Webster defines format briefly as "the shape and size of a book; general style or getup of a book." Under the broad title of "shape and size" we can group all of the mechanical aspects of format.

The physical form of a magazine is governed by whether or not advertising is part of the publishing equation.

In the early days of periodical publishing, the editorial content lived in splendid isolation from the advertising. At first, the ads appeared only on the covers, but gradually they crept inward and occupied confined sections in the front and back of the book. Despite this concession, publishers often decreed that the ads appear on special colored stock to maintain their isolation. The result was a format that resembled a "sandwich," with advertising surrounding a central editorial core. This format is still rather widely used and has the virtue of an uninterrupted editorial section. Its disadvantages rest in the congested

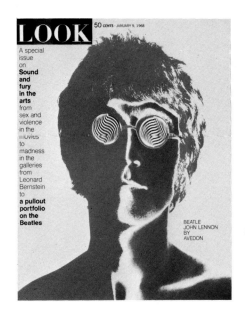

This special issue on "Sound and Fury in the Arts" drew its cohesiveness and continuity from both the subject and the design. The cover upset *Look*'s circulation experts, but its substantial sales success made it clear that attitudes change and no one is a cover expert.

advertising sections in the front and in the necessity of breaking features with continuations. This creates a rather dull catchall area for runover text in the back of the book, an area generally called the "backyard" and often relieved by cartoons or short features.

As advertising took a more respected place in the economics of publishing, it began to spread through the magazine, and editors faced new problems in attracting reader attention and organizing content. This led to a cover-to-cover treatment that is perhaps best described as the "continuous format," which permits each feature to run without interruption except for the intrusion of advertising. It is used by magazines such as *Time* and *The New Yorker* as well as the more visual publications.

The usual plan for a continuous format is: (1) "departments" and advertising in the front; (2) a somewhat reduced editorial core; (3) several subsequent openings of one or more spreads.

This is a difficult format to work with because advertising and editorial content are juxtaposed, and features must be tailored to spaces that are often less than ideal. The format has virtues, however; it often delivers a consistent

The style of the Arts issue depended on a coordinated typographic design and a planned series of strong visual features like Arnold Newman's view of the art scene shown, in part, at the right.

The format for the Arts issue
included a design spectacular
at the center fold. This unit
opened to a forty-inch-wide
double gatefold of the Beatles
by Avedon. On the reverse,
this section included portraits
in solarized color.

pattern of cover-to-cover interest and creates a more exciting overall magazine.

Because continuity of design is so important to any format, it is essential that a designer make every effort to examine layouts and features for a given issue in relation to each other. This is often achieved by grouping full-size or reduced-size stats of each spread on a bulletin board or specially prepared viewing area. These layouts should be as comprehensive as possible, and in a continuous format should include the advertising.

Though magazines are designed and conceived from the front cover to the

The black background of this spread provided a change of pace in the Arts issue. The simple, Mondrian-like division of space was related to the architectural content.

Living in a work of Art

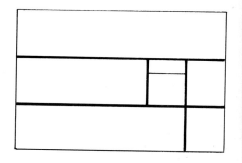

For contrast with the dominant photographic tone of the Arts issue, Saul Steinberg caricatured the supermarkets of culture.

back, all reader habits do not conform to this pattern. Some readers fan the pages in unrelated chunks, and unfortunately too many of them sneak up on designs from behind. In the outer reaches of motivational research someone has probably explored the back-to-front reading phenomenon and is prepared to explain it; but for the designer and editor it is enough to know that it exists.

Awareness of these unorthodox reading habits has influenced magazine format in several ways. Many magazines distribute their highpoints of interest throughout the magazine and often place major features in the final pages. Advertisers have begun to realize that their old preference for front-of-book positions is not as valid as they once believed it to be. Many magazines have ceased relying entirely on the opening unit of a story to capture interest and are using secondary headlines and illustrations on all units of a feature.

Though the erratic reader habits we have been considering are based on subconscious reaction, another aspect of reader approach that has an important influence on format is the conditioned reading pattern, which differs from magazine to magazine. By placing recurring items of interest in the same position in each issue, we can gradually influence the reader's pattern of

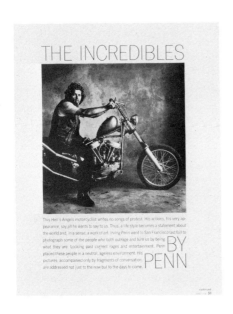

A series of group portraits from California entitled ''The Incredibles'' provided another strong visual accent in the Arts issue. These revealing photographic studies by Irving Penn were posed against a specially built set.

THE SIXTIES

OUR UNBELIEVABLE DECADE

WHAT OTHER TEN YEARS have been so loaded with tragedy, triumph and change? As America hurtles into the Seventies, the mood is very different from what it was in 1960—complacent. Like most of us, I've been shook up, torn apart and exhilarated during the Sixties. I was shaken by assassination after incredible assassination. I was torn to see generation against generation, man against man, white against black. My ears ached with the echo of protest. Protest, PRO-TEST! And I was lifted up, out of myself, purged, when the impossible happened—three men made it to the moon. (The Mets and the moon the same year!)

We are caught in the riptide of two revolutions that started in the Sixties: the young struggling to over-throw the bureaucracy-bound Establishment and the blacks to possess their long-overdue rights. NOW

There has been a determination to cut through the crap, as the young insist on saying. But it has caused some traditions to be ruthlessly jettisoned. The hippie phenomenon, a protest against the fakery and money-mindedness of middle- and upper-class life, has also been a convenient poncho for the lazy and the no-good nik to hide under. School protests became so wide-spread it was obvious some were protesting for the sake of protesting. The revolt against censorship of any kind bared breasts and bottoms of all shapes and sizes, few of them worthy of exposure. It also plopped us into a mud bath of pornography. Some of the cos-tumes worn by the young, including mine, made a stroll in the park a hilarious experience. Ladies' pants-suits, including mine, and male hair became symbols of per-sonal freedom—while in Vietnam the war ground on.

In Appalachia a child starved, in Hollywood a girl walked out of a window because she was high on LSD.

The decade had started so bright-hopefully. When John Fitzgerald Kennedy was inaugurated that windy January day in 1961 (with Robert Frost, bareheaded in the cold, reading a poem), he brought class, cool and culture with him to the White House. He started the Peace Corps. Jackie invited Casals to play. The Presi-dent made a mistake—Cuba—and he promised South Vietnam assistance against Communism. But the young believed.

After less than three years in office, he was shot and killed riding in an open car down a sun-drenched Dallas avenue. Jackie (right, with his brother Robert, Caroline and John) buried him in Arlington as, on TV, the nation watched—and wept.   PATRICIA COFFIN

12 LOOK 1-13-69   PRODUCED BY PATRICIA COFFIN AND ALLEN HURLBURT

This and the examples that follow show how a variety of visual ideas can be woven together without losing the sense of issue continuity.

perusal, but when this is overdone it tends to minimize surprise and leads to an overly rigid format that limits reader interest and excitement.

Magazine format is also affected by changes in patterns of reader interest. Since World War II we have seen general magazines shift from a primary emphasis on entertainment and variety to an emphasis on information and thoroughness. The pretty girl and the entertainment personality no longer dominate covers, and the right words on the cover are often more effective than pictures. Large areas of a magazine — often entire issues — are devoted to a

The Kennedy charisma at its peak. JFK and Jackie relaxing at a White House gala.

Then JFK was gone—the bloody carnation and the magic Pax was swiftly communicated with his young.

THE RISE AND FALL OF   THE HOUSE OF KENNEDY

THE GENERATION CAUGHT BETWEEN VIOLENCE AND EUPHORIA

THE BAD, BEAUTIFUL, MIND-BLOWING YEARS

All photographs do not have
to be large to be effective.
This cluster of fourteen pictures
provides a change of pace within
the section and gains interest
through the varied selection and
careful placement of images.

single subject. This does not mean that general magazines have usurped the role of serious, selective quarterlies, but it does indicate that the balance has shifted and we must find new ways to make serious material provocative and compelling.

The changes that have taken place in the last twenty-five years are important, but they are nothing to what we will face in the decades ahead. The speedup of the educational process through programed instruction and electronic teaching aids, growing emphasis on pure and abstract sciences, increased saturation of our awareness with visual images in an accelerated communication drive — all of these are going to have a momentous influence on the perception of new generations of readers.

As one demonstration of the changes we will face, let us examine the shifting concept of reality. For years, man has accepted a neatly packaged idea of measurable space, fixed time, and a round world that revolves around a reliable sun. Today, science is challenging these three-dimensional views. As we move inward toward the atom and outward toward space, we discover that what seemed unreal to our untrained perception is actually real and what we took for reality is sometimes an illusion.

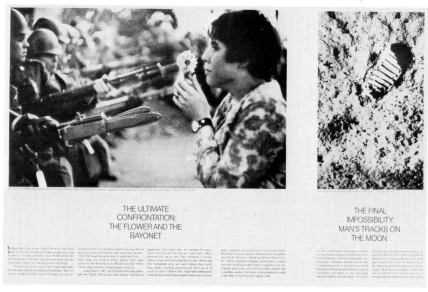

THE ULTIMATE
CONFRONTATION:
THE FLOWER AND THE
BAYONET

THE FINAL
IMPOSSIBILITY:
MAN'S TRACKS ON
THE MOON

Faced with these new concepts, no art director can afford to take his perception and design approach for granted, and no editor can afford the comfortable luxury of editorial formulas and a fixed format. That a format is right for one magazine does not make it right for another, nor is a new format a magic wand that can turn an ailing magazine into an overnight success. Certainly, changes in a poor format can bring it into closer harmony with editorial objectives, and a redirection of editorial ideas in a publication should be accompanied by a corresponding adjustment of the design approach.

The problem of format is never fully resolved. No matter how well a design approach fits the current problems of editorial presentation, it cannot be presumed to be correct for tomorrow's needs. For this reason, perhaps the best attitude toward magazine design is one that accepts continuous change and modification. With such a program, the current issue of a magazine will differ only slightly from the issue before it, but from season to season and year to year a considerable change will be evident.

Technical section

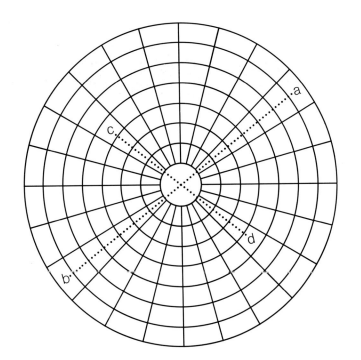

Color theory One of the best-known systems of color notations is the one developed by Dr. Wilhelm Ostwald: it divides a color solid into an outer spectral ring of pure color and an inner axis with white at the top and black at the bottom modifying each of the colors. Ostwald's theories of color harmony stem from two major concepts. The diagram at the top demonstrates the complementary relationship on which the chromatic circle is based (*a* is harmonious with *b* and *c* is harmonious with *d*). The diagram below illustrates the more complex relationship Ostwald describes as the "ring star." When a color is selected at *x*, all the colors along line *a* (isotints), line *b* (isotones), and line *c* will be in harmony. To this Ostwald adds the 24 chromatic divisions that are equidistant from the center.

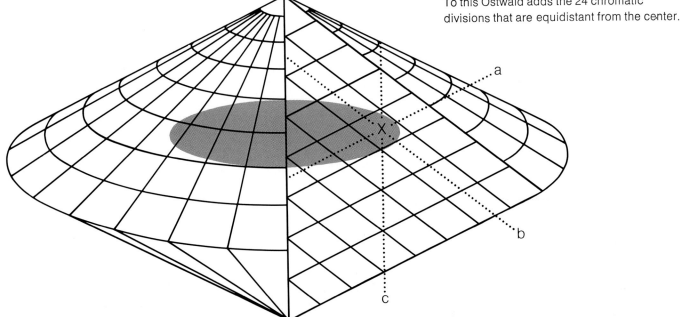

1. Color

Most discussions of color in the graphic arts bog down in the elaborate theories of color harmony. While a knowledge of these theories is certainly valuable to the magazine designer, the creative efforts of many color experts indicate that too much theory can produce dull and unexciting results. Aside from indicating a framework for further color study, this section will concentrate on a few useful facts about color, with particular emphasis on printing.

There are two ways of seeing color. The physicist examining color as light sees it one way. The painter mixing color on his palette, or the printer combining color impressions, sees it differently. Newton, by passing white light through a prism, converted it to a spectrum of colors; then, by passing the spectrum through another prism, reconverted it to white light. He thus established the principle that in light, whiteness is the presence of all colors, and blackness the complete absence of color.

For the designer and printer working in the world of paper and pigment, the opposite is true. Whiteness for our purposes is the absence of color, and blackness the sum of all colors. Thus, the beautiful blacks of a color transparency are arrived at by a combination of three color dyes — cyan, magenta, and yellow. (Actually, the technical limitations of the printing process require that black be treated as a separate color, and we will treat it here in this manner.)

Color selection   Though a study of theory and notation may be helpful in understanding color, the selection of color for a design is most frequently a subjective decision based on personal taste. A skilled designer can defy all of the carefully worked out rules of the psychologists and color theorists and create exciting results.

Contrast in color   A given color appears darker on a light background, lighter on a dark background, warmer on a cool background, and cooler on a warm background. In the illustration below, the gray bar is constant in value, but it appears darker against the light area, and lighter against the dark area.

It should be remembered that the white of the whitest paper and the black of the blackest ink are never absolute black and white. This is demonstrated when we compare a color transparency against the printed color. The white light that comes through the transparency will be far whiter than the paper, and the printed picture will seem flat in comparison.

The psychology of color sensation   Though many complex theories of reaction to color have been devised, most of the findings are inconclusive and present unnecessary obstacles to the designer. Aside from the rather obvious associations of color in nature — the red of fire, sunset, and blood; the blue of sky and water; the yellow of sunlight and wheat; the green of grass and leaves — color meaning is as elusive as scientific color harmony.

Color control   The problem does not end with the selection of images and the layout of the pages. Because the success of the color will be finally judged by its printed impression, the designer has an obligation to understand the printing process and to work closely with the technicians who are responsible for it.

The designer's awareness of what is involved in reproduction should begin

Care in copy preparation
and quality control in
production are essential
to the design process.

with picture selection. When 35 mm. slides are projected in the darkened viewing room, one can easily be lulled into a false sense of security. Pictures have a way of looking sharper and more glamorous in this environment than they can ever be on the printed page. This is not meant to diminish the importance of this technique of picture editing, which allows you, with the aid of a zoom lens, to actually size pictures into the page; it is only meant as a warning.

Before final selections are made, the transparencies should be checked on a lightbox, under a high magnification viewer. They should also be enlarged photographically (in color if the budget permits) to final image size for a further test of their reproduction potential.

While quality duplication is expensive, it can sometimes even save money on a spread where several images are to be combined, by eliminating the expensive stripping cost that the engraver or printer will otherwise charge.

When images are enlarged, either by duplication or for reproduction, certain changes take place. There is a reduction in contrast and a general opening up of the darker values. Enlargement will also fully reveal flaws in focus and film resolution.

Many forms of transparency and print film are available. For extreme enlargements, Kodachrome II delivers the best resolution and, hence, the best reproduction. Other films, especially negative-print film, yield a less precise result, but these often faster films can work well when the degree of enlargement is not great, or when photographic grain is not a problem.

It has been my experience that printers in all processes create better results from transparencies than from opaque photographic color prints of any type. One reason is that they have more extensive experience with transparencies today. Another is that the transparency reveals details in the dense areas that are often blocked out in a color print.

The ultimate test and final control of reproduction is in the reading and correcting of proofs. This is a difficult and highly technical process. The designer must learn to work closely with production experts and try to understand their problems. It is important that the designer and the engraver or printer look at the same thing. Your lightboxes should match his lightboxes, and the overhead lights should be as similar as possible. A comparison of the way any color proof looks under fluorescent light and under tungsten light will demonstrate why this is important.

In studying hundreds of color proofs, I have observed one fact worth noting here. When going over progressive proofs, study the top sheet, which includes all colors, and compare it carefully with the original before looking at the separate color proofs. The proofs of individual colors, or combinations of two or three colors, can confuse even the color expert, and sometimes lead to erroneous correction.

Though most color correction and examination take place in a controlled, somewhat clinical atmosphere, it is a good idea to also look at some proofs under the kind of lighting conditions in which they will eventually be viewed: daylight through a window, normal reading light, and the fluorescent glare of the market where the magazine may be displayed and sold. Remember that color is a vital experience, and we should not become so involved in clinical matching that we ignore its ultimate effect.

2. The grid

In the second chapter of this book, on the elements of page design, I discussed the relation of the grid or modular design system to the design process. Because this approach to page and format design is playing an increasingly important role in the design and makeup of modern magazines, this chapter will explore the grid and its application in more detail.

Without even knowing it, most magazines use a grid system in the layout of their pages. The preprinted sheets that mark the page dimensions, column widths, and margins fall into this category, but without design considerations these grid sheets become self-limiting. The creative key to the success of a designer's grid is the carefully planned relationship of the horizontal and vertical divisions of space and the proportions it generates. This brings a completely modular control to the design of the pages without limiting the essential flexibility of the format. When it works, the grid accommodates a wide variety of features, all types and sizes of illustrations, and allows for a finished design with either a vertical or horizontal emphasis.

In determining the best proportions for a grid, the designer may depend entirely on his perception and intuitive judgment, or he may base his system on established rules governing the division of space. His options include the square, the double square, and the golden mean as expressed in Le Corbusier's modular referred to in Chapter 3. Carefully worked out proportions are no guarantee of exciting pages, and the final success of the grid will be measured by the dynamics of the layouts it generates.

In the earlier discussion of the grid some of the advantages and disadvantages of this approach to page design were reviewed. There will always be

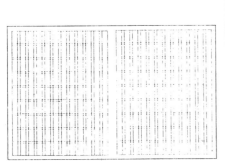

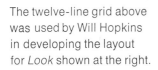

The twelve-line grid above
was used by Will Hopkins
in developing the layout
for *Look* shown at the right.

times when you will want to free yourself, your photographer, or your illustrator
from all restrictions and use the total space with complete freedom. There will be
other times when a cohesive system will permit you to use a wide range of
material and create exciting design solutions within the framework of the grid.

On the opposite page, a single grid system has been developed to show how
this approach can be applied to a magazine format. The grid is planned to
accommodate either a two-column or three-column makeup. It also provides
on one side of the page a wide margin which can serve as a separation between
editorial and advertising content. The horizontal divisions of space create a
modular system that is based on the square but flexible enough to accommodate visual units of various sizes and proportions. No single grid system can
be appropriate to all magazines, or for the visual ideas of all designers, and this
demonstration is only intended to suggest one approach to magazine design.

Today, the relentless advance of technology and the increasing economic
pressure on magazines is creating a new reason for supporting the grid.
Computer photo-typesetting and film assembly of page elements call for
simplified procedures in the preparation of copy for reproduction. Massimo

The grid pattern shown in one-quarter scale (right) and with a layout superimposed (above) is designed for the 8½″ by 11″ page size with a two- and three-column option. It represents only one of many possible design solutions.

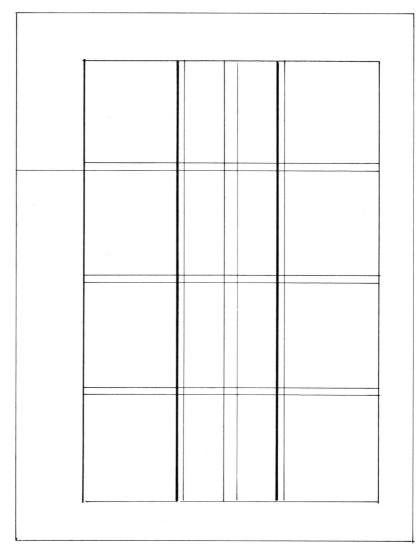

Vignelli, a designer who has applied the grid to a wide range of graphic problems, was one of the first to point out that a well-organized grid system provides the order and simplicity that is essential to modern reproduction methods.

It was inevitable that in the new technology of magazine production some of the steps in the process of copy preparation would be eliminated. Today, on a growing number of magazines, rough visuals drawn to a grid are being translated directly into press-ready pages by technicians. Film replaces photostats and type proofs, and the light table serves as a substitute for the drawing board in a procedure that ends in negative film assembly without the benefit of a paste-up mechanical. It is easy to see how the accuracy of a predetermined grid can aid such a process.

The noted Swiss designer Josef Muller-Brockman, an exponent of design systems, sums up the advantage of this approach when he says, "The grid makes it possible to bring together all of the elements of design — typography, photography, and drawings — into harmony with each other. The grid process is a means of introducing order into design." Le Corbusier, the man most responsible for the modular approach of contemporary design adds this note of caution: "I still reserve the right at any time to doubt the solutions furnished by the modular, keeping intact my freedom which must depend on my feelings rather than my reason."

3. Typography

The Trajan inscriptions

There is increasing evidence that masses of people are no longer looking to magazines for escape, but are seeking in them a greater understanding of the complex world in which we live. This means that the publication designer must be increasingly aware of words, their meaning, and their visual language — typography.

Throughout this book I have emphasized the use of simple solutions to

91

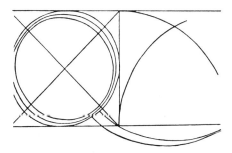

These classic drawings from the fifteenth century suggest the Renaissance revival of interest in Roman inscriptions.

design problems. In no other area is simplicity so important as in type selection and type specification.

Typography itself is an extremely complex process. Not only are hundreds of typefaces in existence, but there are an incredible number of variations within these typefaces: roman, italic, light, medium, bold, ultra- or extrabold, plus varying degrees of letter condensation and expansion. Add to these the various methods of setting type: Linotype, Intertype, Monotype, and Ludlow in metal, and now a dozen different systems of electronic and photographic typesetting, and you begin to realize how staggering the options are.

Most of the text in this book is set in Helvetica, yet there are many typefaces that look almost exactly like it to any but the most expert eye — Akzidenz, Univers, Venus, Folio, Grotesque, Standard, Trade Gothic, and Lightline Gothic, to name a few.

In this chapter I will attempt to bring some order out of the chaos of hot- and cold-type composition, but it is impossible to adequately describe here all the systems that exist for turning manuscript copy into printed pages. There are two main systems by which the bulk of modern magazine body copy is set: Linotype and computer compositon.

Linotype (a hot-metal process) This is still the most commonly used system. A keyboard guides type matrices into a form from which a line slug is cast. The lines are then put together into paragraphs and columns and proved with ink on paper. Linotype is fast, reasonably economical, and not difficult to correct, and it offers a large range of typefaces.

Computer composition (the cold-type process) In computer typesetting the keyboard perforates a tape that activates a computer-controlled machine that

Hot- and cold-type composition

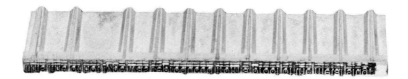

This line of hot type was reproduced from a proof of the metal slug.

This line of cold type was reproduced from a photographic print.

A comparison of the principal
methods of type composition is
demonstrated in this illustration.
The line of hot type is shown with
a picture of the Linotype slug
from which it was printed, and a
similar line of cold type is shown
with the punched tape that
generated its ultimate printout.

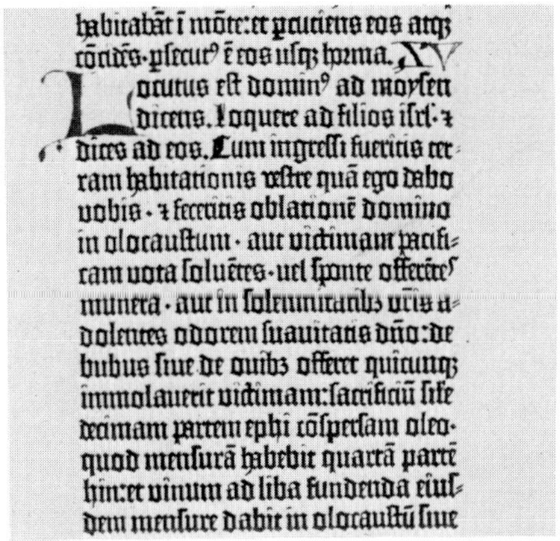

Gutenberg's type was based
on the Gothic style in 1440,
but Nicolas Jenson was guided
by the humanistic script in
developing the letters at the
right only thirty years later.

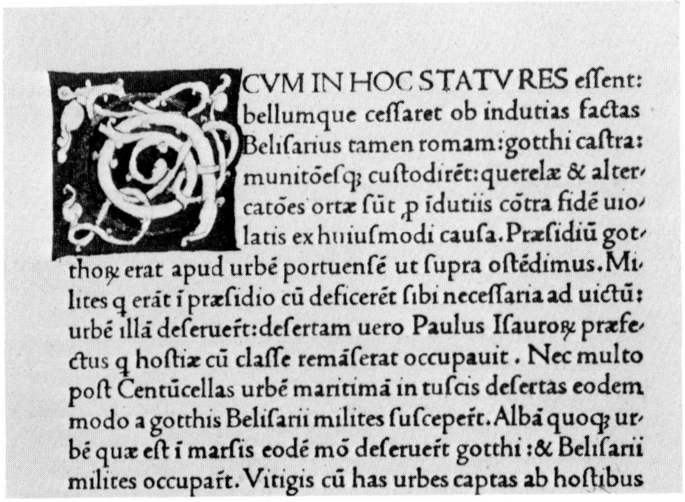

rapidly exposes the letters through grids on negative film. The result is then
assembled and photographically printed. This system is amazingly fast and
potentially more economical than hot type, and the printout of the letters is
extremely sharp. Cold type is complex because it is new and because there is
very little compatibility among the many systems now in use. A present
weakness lies in the limited availability of well-drawn letter forms, but many

systems are making rapid progress in this area. Composition also can be more expensive than hot type if extensive corrections are required, but wider use of the tape-merger system will probably overcome this problem eventually.

One difference between hot and cold type that is of particular interest to the designer is the variety of results from the two proving methods. Most typefaces were originally designed for the letterpress impression on paper. The photographic printout produces a sharper and cleaner image, but it has a slightly different color and texture. The classic book designer will be more concerned by the difference than the magazine art director, who will often find that the advantages of tighter spacing and clear, uniform images outweigh this minor imperfection.

The preceding paragraphs indicate the complexity of the typographic process, but the publication designer need not use or even understand all of the resources available. It is possible to do an effective publication format with a single typeface if enough sizes are available and if the type includes a bold face and an italic. The specimens on page 103 show varied forms of two of the typefaces most frequently used for magazine text. You may be tempted to reject these out of hand because of their overexposure, but remember that the style and distinction of a format is not determined by the precise shape of the characters of a ten-point alphabet.

Type legibility   Many studies have been made of the comparative legibility of typefaces, and each has come up with fractional advantages for one type over another. Many magazines have thrived with words set in less than ideal type, and others have expired with type of scientifically proven legibility. The answer seems to lie in good words and in the art director's sound, but not necessarily scientific, judgment. Perhaps overall readability is a more important yardstick. If the look of the page and its content is sufficiently interesting to the reader, he will read it.

The anatomy of type   Since Gutenberg, type has been cast in metal with a body and a face. The height of the type body determines its size — 6-point, 10-point, etc. — and it is identified by its face: Bodoni, Caslon, Times Roman, etc. In addition, most typefaces have the following variations: roman and italic, regular weight and bold face; some types, particularly the modern sans serifs, have extended and condensed forms as well as many variations in weight.

The basic type families   There are many ways of dividing typefaces into groups. Some type experts use as many as ten or twenty classifications, but for the sake of simplicity, I will group them into three families:

Old style

When the printers of Mainz made their historic introduction of movable type, they based their designs on the gothic letters that dominated German manuscripts. It remained for the punch cutters of fifteenth century Venice, particularly Jenson and Griffo, to design and cut the first alphabets in the roman style we know today. Though their capital letters retained a close relationship to the great inscriptions of the Romans, the lowercase was based on the calligraphic forms that had been used for centuries. The quill strokes influenced the form of the serifs and the off-center weighting of the curved strokes that are still characteristic of the old-style typefaces of our day.

Though typefaces such as Bembo, Poliphilus, and Centaur most closely follow the patterns cut in Venice, many faces, including some new ones, can be fitted into the old-style category. Among these are: Garamond, Caslon, Times Roman, and Palatino.

Modern

Just as the old-style typefaces were born in the classic revival of the Renaissance, the type we have known as "modern" for over two hundred years was designed in the neoclassic formalism of the eighteenth century. The Italian, Giambattista Bodoni, designed an alphabet that abandoned the influence of calligraphy and returned to the inscribed letters of early Rome for the crisp characteristics of its shading and serifs. In the same century, Firmin Didot (one of the family of famous French typographers) designed a very similar alphabet. The modern group of typefaces also includes Baskerville and Bulmer (sometimes classified as transitional), as well as Century, Scotch Roman, Caledonia, Walbaum, and Torino.

Structural

With the development of mechanization and the emphasis on engineering in the nineteenth century, structural letter forms appeared. These typefaces, not based on calligraphy or inscription, were attempts to solve the typographic needs of posters rather than books.

For over five centuries, most headlines have been reproduced from handset foundry type. This method is illustrated by the four letters of 72-point Caslon positioned above the proof of the letters (right). Most typographic nomenclature and many rules of composition are based on this system, but today an increasing volume of display type is reproduced from photographic film.

The anatomy of a typeface

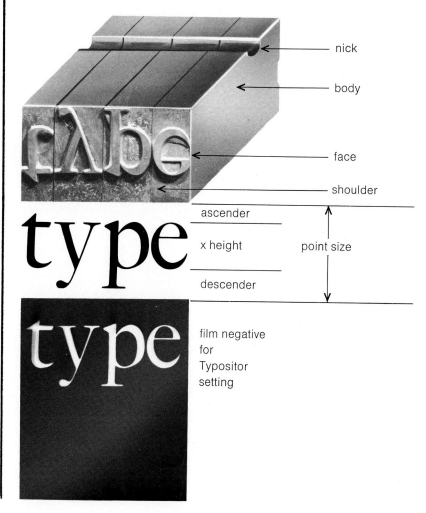

nick

body

face

shoulder

ascender

x height

descender

point size

film negative
for
Typositor
setting

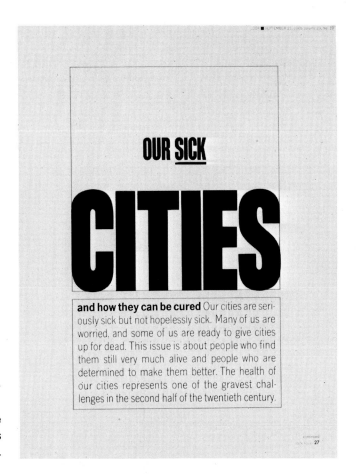

Simple and articulate typography often creates its own design solution.

This family includes the many sans-serif types generally classified as gothics or grotesques, such as Franklin Gothic, News Gothic, Futura, Helvetica, etc. Classified as structural letters are also some sans-serif faces with thick and thin strokes, like Optima and Peignot, and square-serif faces sometimes called Egyptians: Clarendon, Beton, Stymie, and even those Circus faces that Dr. Agha once described as serif-sans-type: Barnum and Playbill.

Structural letter forms do not offer the warmth or large-area legibility of the

98

A bleed picture is often a desirable design objective, but a type bleed can be a disaster. Here the effect is deliberate and successful.

old-style and modern faces, but they have a simplicity and strength that is consistent with contemporary attitudes toward design.

From the three major classifications described in the preceding paragraphs come practically all of the commonly used text faces and most display type. There are some notable exceptions. The Old English typefaces have their origin in the Germanic alphabet, and most script faces are based on Spencerian and other handwriting. Other faces are occasionally drawn from combinations of one or more of the roots described.

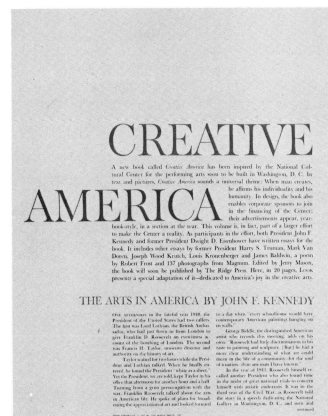

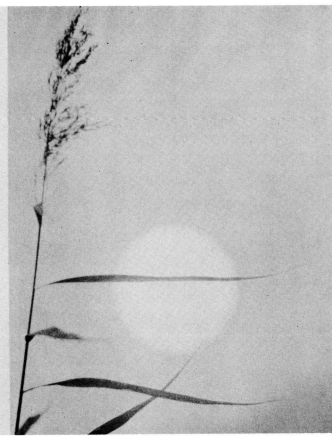

Headlines need not always
appear above the text.
In this design the title and
text were treated as a
single plastic element.

Type measurement   Although printing was introduced in the fifteenth century, it was not until two hundred years later that a uniform method of type measurement was devised. Firmin Didot worked out the point system, which formed the basis for type measurement.

The point system in use today in America prescribes 12 points to a pica and approximately 6 picas to the inch. Type sizes are designated by points, and measurements of type areas are normally designated in picas.

The em and the en are variable measurements normally used for indentation

100

Sometimes a cover design is best served by type alone as this cover of *Avant Garde* designed by Herb Lubalin demonstrates. The typeface created for the logotype became a designers' favorite.

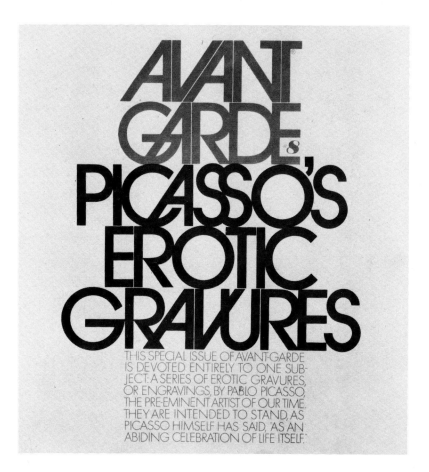

and spacing. The em is a square of a given type size; the en is half as much. A one-em indent in a paragraph of 12-point type equals 12 points; in 10-point type it equals 10 points.

Because type size is based on the body of the type rather than the face, point size can be a misleading measurement. For example, the letter *O* in 8-point Times Roman is large enough to encompass the *O* in 10-point Caslon 471. This difference is caused by variations in the length of the ascenders and descenders in the different typefaces. Type is often described as having a large or a small *x* height, which is the size of the lowercase *x* in relation to the overall size of the typeface.

Type color   Three factors determine the "color" or texture of a type area: the weight of the typeface, the amount of leading (space between the lines), and the relation of the type to the impression that the printing process delivers and to the quality of the printing surface.

Text typography   Though there are dozens of typefaces that can be used for setting text, five dominate in magazines today. They are Bodoni Book, Baskerville, Times Roman, Century, and Helvetica (or one of its cousins).

Bodoni Book is a modification of the original Bodoni design. It sets rather narrow and has sufficiently long ascenders and descenders so that it can be set with minimum leading. Its overall color is rather light and even.

Baskerville is a transitional typeface. It is similar to Bodoni Book in color, but the letters are rounder and slightly larger. Its most notable characteristic is the open lower loop in the lowercase g.

Times Roman was developed in the 1930s after extensive experiments for the venerable London *Times*. In spite of its twentieth-century origin, its roots are firmly planted in the tradition of old-style types. The form of the serifs, the off-center weight distribution on the curves of the lowercase letters, and the relation of thick and thin all stem from the humanistic letter forms of the Renaissance. It differs from them, however, in its shortened ascenders and descenders — a concession to modern copyfitting problems — and in its attention to legibility. Because of this, Times Roman has larger letters, size for size, than most other serif type, but it does not fit so compactly and it needs more leading.

Century Expanded is a very open face, drawn for high legibility. It has short ascenders and descenders. Its color is similar to that of Bodoni Book and Baskerville, but its *x* height is closer to that of Times Roman.

Helvetica Light is the only sans-serif type covered in this list of text faces. As noted earlier, there are several other similar faces with different names.

102

Text composition

THE POWER OF WORDS They sing. They hurt. They teach. They sanctify. They were man's first, immeasurable feat of magic. They liberated us from ignorance and our barbarous past. For without these marvelous scribbles which build letters into words, words into sentences, sentences into systems and sciences and creeds, man would be forever confined to the self-isolated prison of the scuttle-fish or the chimpanzee.

The power of words They sing. They hurt. They teach. They sanctify. They were man's first, immeasurable feat of magic. They liberated us from ignorance and our barbarous past. For without these marvelous scribbles which build letters into words, words into sentences, sentences into systems and sciences and creeds, man would be forever confined to the self-isolated prison of the scuttlefish . . .

WE LIVE BY WORDS: *love, truth, God.* We fight for words: *freedom, country, fame.* We die for words: *liberty, glory, honor.* They bestow the priceless gift of articulacy on our minds and hearts — from "Mama" to "infinity." And the men who truly shape our destiny, the giants who teach us, inspire us, lead us to deeds of immortality are those who use words with clarity, grandeur and passion: Socrates, Jesus, Luther, Lincoln, Churchill.

These words by Leo Rosten are set in four different text styles on this page. The type at the left is 9-point Times Roman with 1-point lead, 13 picas wide (usually specified 9/10 x 13). At this width there are 37 characters to the line, and at this width and leading, about 46 words to each column inch.

The type above is 10-point Times Roman with 1-point lead, 20 picas wide (usually specified 10/11 x 20). This is set with a three-line dropped initial. At this width there are 53 characters to the line, and at this width and leading there are about 66 words to each column inch.

The type at the left is 9-point Helvetica light with 1-point lead, 13 picas wide (usually specified 9/10 x 13). At this width there are 36 characters to the line, and at this width and leading, about 44 words to each column inch.

The type below is 9-point Helvetica light with 2-point lead, 20 picas wide (usually specified 9/11 x 20). This is set with a raised initial in 42-point Stymie Bold Condensed. At this width and leading there are about 69 words to each column inch.

WE live by words: *love, truth, God.* We fight for words: *freedom, country, fame.* We die for words: *liberty, glory, honor.* They bestow the priceless gift of articulacy on our minds and hearts — from "Mama" to "infinity." And the men who truly shape our destiny, the giants who teach us, inspire us, lead us to deeds of immortality are those who use words with clarity, grandeur and passion: Socrates, Jesus, Luther, Lincoln, Churchill.

103

Helvetica

Helvetica

Helvetica

Helvetica

Helvetica

Helvetica

Helvetica

Helvetica

Helvetica is a recent face based on grotesque style. It is a simple structural letter that has many uses. It is shown here in a few variations of weight.

Helvetica has the largest *x* height of any face mentioned here, and its ascenders and descenders are very short. Because of its large x height, Helvetica is generally used in a smaller size than other faces, but a reasonable amount of leading is necessary.

Copyfitting   There are two basic methods of fitting copy to the text areas of a magazine. One approximates length by using word count as a guide. The other, more accurate, method is based on character count.

A rough word count may be arrived at by estimating the number of words to a typewritten page (200–300 words per double-spaced page, depending on type size, margins, etc.) and multiplying this by the number of manuscript pages. Next, the average number of words per column-width line and the number of lines per inch of the specified type are determined. By multiplying these, the average number of words per column inch is obtained. This divided into the total number of words in the manuscript gives the approximate length of the typeset article in column inches.

For close copyfitting, and for captions and self-contained copy blocks, it is wise to use the more accurate method of character counting. (It is helpful to know that a typewriter equipped with elite type sets twelve characters to the inch, while pica type counts ten characters to the inch. The only exception is the ''executive'' typewriter, which has variable character widths that require an averaging of the character count. Many magazines with standard column measures provide writers with copy paper indicating the length of line to typewrite in order to match the typeset lines.) The average number of characters to a given amount of a selected typeface and size is determined easily by referring to one of the many charts available in type books or from compositors; this divided into the total number of characters in the manuscript gives the length fairly closely.

Copyfitting is one of the mechanical problems that publication designers face in the process of layout. It is not difficult, but like any mechanical skill, it requires a certain amount of practice.

Once a magazine art director has become experienced in fitting typewritten copy to the type page, he will find that he can make quick estimates of the space that text will occupy and the number of lines a caption may require. His intuitive judgments will make it possible to combine words with visual elements in the early stages of layout planning, although the estimates will probably require

Futura Light

Futura Book

Futura Medium

Futura Demi

Futura Bold

Futura Ex

Futura Black

Futura Display

Futura, designed by Paul Renner in 1925 and used by *Vanity Fair* in 1929, has proven to be one of the most durable typefaces of our time. Only a few of its many options are shown above.

Bodoni Book

Bodoni

Bodoni Bold

Ultra Bodoni

Bauer Bodoni

Bauer Bodoni

The Bodoni shown at the top is the most commonly used design, but the Bauer version is more like the original. Firmin Didot (below) is little changed after two centuries.

Firmin Didot

Firmin Didot

No one knows exactly how many different typefaces exist. Here is a random selection that only hints at the many choices that are available. The selection begins with old style and then continues through transitional to modern and miscellaneous faces.

Garamond

Garamond

Times Roman

Times Roman

Janson

Janson Italic

Baskerville

Century

more careful, mechanical measurements as the layout progresses.

Picture captions　Captions may be set in many different ways. When picture layouts first came to the printed page, the captions were set in neat rectangles below the picture, with all lines of equal length. In recent years, the trend has been to less formal styles, with captions set flush left or flush right. Italic is often used to give captions an informal or conversational tone.

Sometimes it is easier for the designer to group his captions away from the pictures and to identify them with key numbers or notations such as "upper right," "lower left." This makes a lot of extra work for the reader, however, and since the designer is paid and the reader is not, it is a habit to be avoided.

Most readers expect pictures to have captions, and it is a good rule to include them. The rule will sometimes be broken, but each exception should be approached with thought.

Display typography　In choosing display type, the designer is dealing with the headlines, the selling words that are planned to create reader interest. These words should be studied and analyzed, first for their meaning and second for typographic considerations.

There are many ways to approach display typography on the printed page. In some publications, particularly where text dominates the content, a uniform style is set and maintained. This approach can be used effectively in a more pictorial format as well. In other magazines, display typography is treated with complete freedom, and each new headline is approached as a typographic exercise. This too can be effective, but it requires great skill and great control on the part of the designer to maintain continuity and to prevent confusion of advertising and editorial matter. Most successful visual formats compromise between these two approaches by establishing a basic type style for part of the content and elsewhere using other display faces with considerable freedom to achieve variety and the all-important change of pace.

The metal body of a hot-type letter makes its own boundaries, separating letter from letter and line from line. Today, however, scissors and the camera have made it possible to manipulate type with extraordinary freedom. Letters can be interlocked, compressed, made wider, narrower, darker, or lighter, and slanted in any direction and at almost any angle by photographic means. Type can serve as a pictorial element, and new emphasis can be placed on words by

Modern No.20

Optima

Kabel Bold

Avant Garde

PRISMA

Peignot Medium

Bookman

Egyptian

Clarendon

Bank Script

graphic distortion. To be effective, these devices must be used with skill and restraint. Overdone or crudely executed, they become self-conscious tricks and tend to destroy the very effect they were meant to achieve.

Hand-lettering and photolettering   In general, when a designer is faced with choosing between hand-lettering and type, he is well advised to pick the time-tested letter forms developed by such experts as Bodoni, Didot, Caslon, and Baskerville. A few expert letterers are contributing to the freedom and flexibility of the printed page today, but most designers use hand-lettering sparingly and usually choose photographic lettering when metal type cannot solve the problem.

Photographic systems for setting display type, such as the Typositor, use either a type or hand-lettered alphabet (frequently equipped with alternate characters) and compose it on photographic paper. Faster than hand-lettering, photolettering is also more flexible than metal display type, because the size variations are unlimited and weight, slant, width, and spacing can be altered almost at will.

Typographic standards   Rules and regulations are never an adequate substitute for the designer's experience, good taste, and creative capacity. The following standards represent a summary of good typographic practice that can only serve the designer as a guide in a complicated area.

Text type
1. For years it has been maintained that the ideal measure for type is one and one-half alphabets to a line. This rule is too rigid for practical purposes, but large areas of lines of less than twenty-five or more than eighty characters should be avoided. Lines under twenty-five characters long result in poor spacing, and excessively long lines are difficult to read.

2. For legibility, long lines normally need more leading than short lines.

3. Text should always have close word spacing. It is better to break words than to have gaps within the line. Word spaces should be about the equivalent of the letter *i*.

4. When initial letters are used, they should fit into a rectangular indentation; their base should align with the last line of indented copy and their top should align with the top of the copy unit or extend above it. When the initial is *A* or *L*,

107

fiffihknꞥrrꞥwwꞥy

AAABCꞬDEFGHIJ

KKLMMMꞰNNꞱPRR

RꞦSSSTꞮUVWXYY

$&.,-:;'""?!()*/%Ɡ&$¢¢

The alternate letter forms and ligatures of one photo version of Bookman Italic hint at the range of typographic options.

the first line of text should generally be longer than the other indented lines. Small capitals are often used for the lead words following an initial. When an initial is used to divide text areas, a minimum of one line of space should separate the units.

5. If available, small capitals are recommended for abbreviations such as US, UN, UNESCO, etc., and the periods should be omitted.

6. It is good form not to indent the first paragraph of a text unit or the first paragraph after a subheading. The normal paragraph indentation is one em, but this may be increased, particularly if the lines are long.

7. In some advertising copy, paragraphs are not indented, and the separation is achieved by inserting extra space between the paragraphs. Though this method is occasionally used in publications, it should generally be avoided when large areas of type are involved.

8. The term *widow* is used to describe a single word on the last line of a paragraph. Widows should be eliminated by editing copy, particularly if they consist of only one syllable or fall at the top or bottom of a column.

Caption type

1. In squared-up captions (justified on both margins), all lines should be carefully written to fit the space. Short last lines and lines forced to fit by word-

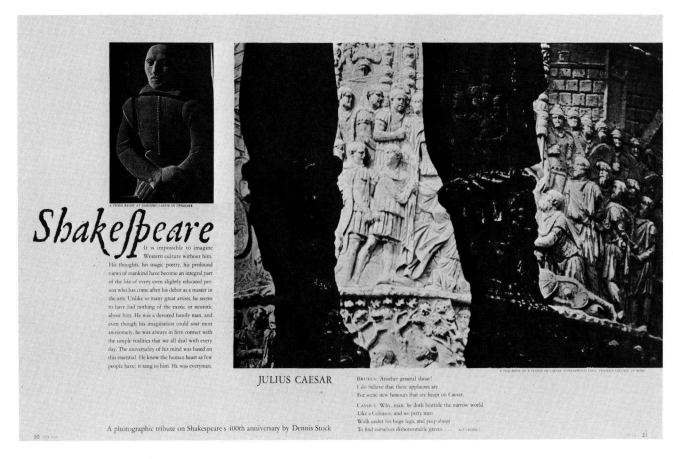

A photographic tribute on Shakespeare's 400th anniversary by Dennis Stock

The type for the "Shakespeare" headline is a photographic enlargement from the First Folio edition.

or letter-spacing should be avoided.

2. In flush-left captions, the designer's eye must judge the spacing of the right-hand margin. In general, excessive discrepancy in line lengths and long first and last lines are to be avoided.

3. Flush-right captions should be used sparingly. The eye has difficulty finding line beginnings in this arrangement, and lengthy captions set to a wide measure are almost impossible to read.

109

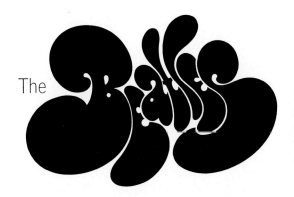

The

In spite of all the type and film alphabets that are available, there are still times when hand-lettering offers the best solution.

Display type

1. It is an archaic form to capitalize the first letter of each headline word. A line with normal capitalization looks better and is easier to read.

2. When a headline is set in more than one line, every effort should be made to break the line into reading phrases. Reading it out loud will indicate where the best divisions are.

3. A lowercase headline should generally be set without letter-spacing and with tight word-spacing.

4. A headline set in all capitals should normally be set tight, but in some cases letter-spacing may be required to make the letters look properly spaced. The letter-spacing should not be mechanically equal, but should be optically balanced.

5. When capitals of varying sizes are used in the same layout, the spacing in each size should be optically equal.

A sound knowledge of typography and typographic standards is only part of the story. The designer will benefit by being constantly aware of who the reader is, of his motivation and his reading habits. Young designers, for instance, often forget that an 8-point letter looks a lot larger to them than to the reader who is over forty. Above all, words are to be read. A publication designer who reads the words he works with will not only improve his relations with his editor, but will be in a better position to find meaningful solutions to design problems.

110

4. Layout and production

While draftsmanship is important in all areas of art direction, the publication designer is rarely required to render finished layouts. His ideas are frequently laid out in the roughest kind of "thumbnail" sketches done on the back of an envelope, in the white space of someone else's ad in his morning newspaper, or on a miniature grid sheet. This approach has the advantage of permitting maximum creative freedom — no one has ever been able to draw a photograph of an event that has not yet occurred — and these sketches often serve as the only guide for a photographer and illustrator.

The rough layout   When the photographs have been completed and the headlines written, a plan is drawn to fit the actual space. This serves as the "blueprint" for the printed page. Little time is devoted to rendering the photographic areas, but careful attention is given to the spaces, typography, proportion, and photographic cropping.

The comprehensive   The comprehensive layout translates the rough into a reasonable facsimile of the printed page. Photostats or photoprints of the pictures are mounted in position. Dummy type is used for the type areas, and headlines are either set in type or carefully rendered.

At this stage the layout and feature can be appraised by the editors. The design is not always final: it may be redone or modified many times.

All publications may not be able to execute the comprehensive layout as outlined. Time and cost limitations may require shortcuts, but this procedure is the best way to achieve a polished and coordinated magazine design.

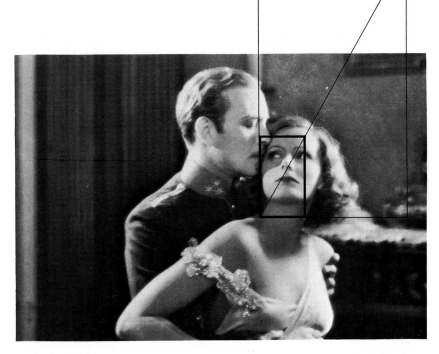

Fitting the picture to the layout   After a photograph has been selected and a general space provided for it in the layout, it may be fitted in several ways.

1. Perhaps the quickest way to fit a picture is to place a corner of the cropped image in the corner of the layout space it is to occupy and draw a line from the corner of the image through the corner diagonally opposite. A rectangle completed at any point along this line will be in proportion to the rectangle indicated on the photograph. At this stage either the layout space or the cropping can be modified.

2. There are several commercial proportionate slide rules that will mechanically translate a rectangle to a smaller or larger image of the same proportion. There are also several enlarging devices for instantaneously tracing a picture into a space of any size.

All of these methods are helpful, but none of them is as valuable as the trained eye that can almost instinctively place pictures properly on the page in the rectangular shape that makes maximum use of the photographic content and the design.

When the visual material for a layout is in itself spectacular, a restrained

Sometimes the essential image can exist within a picture. Here a new view of Garbo was discovered in a rather tired, overused photograph that was enlarged along the diagonal to create a dramatic portrait for the layout (above).

design is often the best framework for presenting it. It is only when the material is ordinary that the publication designer needs to call on his full resources for imaginative cropping and graphic effect. The layout reproduced on this page presented such a problem. (Most of the layouts reproduced in this book are from *Look* because it is simpler for me to explain my own motives and procedures than to attempt to interpret the intentions of other designers. To provide some balance, I have included in this chapter several designs from a wide range of contemporary magazines.)

The four spreads shown
above are the work of
Will Hopkins, who became art
director of *Look* in 1968.

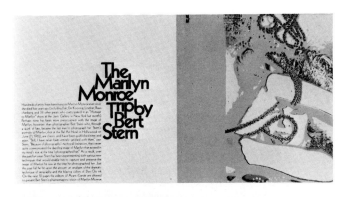

Herb Lubalin created the
spreads at the left for
Avant Garde magazine.
The layouts above were
designed by Bea Feitler,
who shared the art direction
of *Harper's Bazaar* with
Ruth Ansel in the sixties.

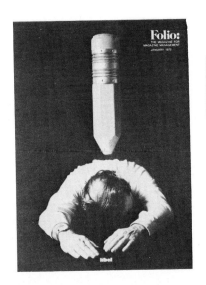

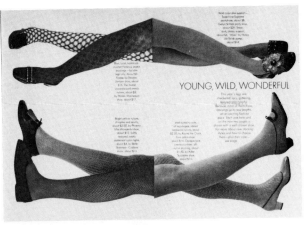

The award-winning cover for *Folio* magazine (top) and the spread from *New Times,* an innovative news magazine, were created by Steve Phillips.

Redbook has maintained a consistently high standard of design under the art direction of William Cadge.

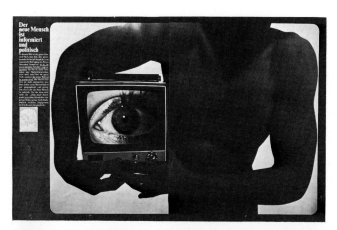

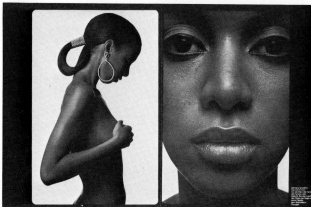

Willy Fleckhaus produced these
two effective layouts for
Twen, a German publication.

The business publication cover
at the top was designed by
Ivan Chermayeff to emphasize
structural strength. The spread
above is from *Ameryka*, a USIA
publication that goes to Poland.
Dave Moore is art director.

David Hillman
created this cover
and spread for
Nova, a magazine
that was as much
a part of the
London scene as
Carnaby Street.

The cover for *Psychology
Today* and the spread with
artwork by Bill Buerge
were art directed and
designed by Tom Gould.

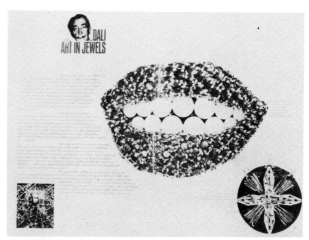

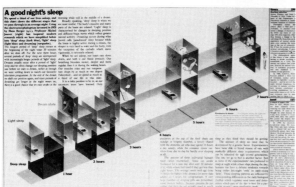

Mineral Digest ,
art directed by
Robert Sadler, and
*Emergency
Medicine*, designed
by Tom Lennon, are
highly specialized
publications.

The London *Sunday Times
Magazine* mixes bold journalism
with graphic presentation
of informative articles under
art director Michael Rand.

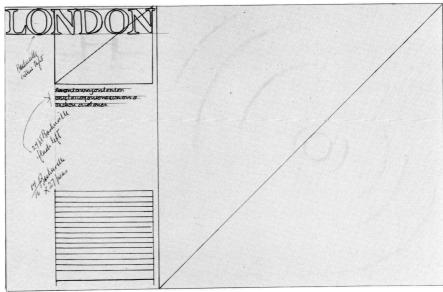

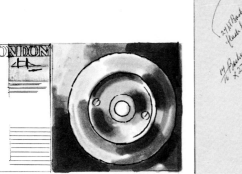

The thumbnail sketch above
and the rough sketch at right
were steps in the creation of
the spread reproduced on
the opposite page.

Magazine covers   It is very difficult to make a general statement concerning covers. What is correct for one magazine may be totally wrong for another. Some publications use a graphic, sometimes abbreviated, presentation of the table of contents. Others rely on dramatic pictures that may or may not be related to the content of the specific issue. The extent to which a magazine relies on newsstand sales will have an influence on the cover approach, but in the competition for reader time, a magazine cover must sell itself on the office desk or coffee table as well as the newsstand.

Many studies of cover effectiveness have been made, but they have provided very few answers. If all factors of content and emotional appeal are equal, a simple but strong poster quality increases the effectiveness of the cover. A picture with words that sell the content of the magazine does better than the picture alone on most magazines, but a busy, junky cover may damage the image the designer is attempting to create.

LONDON

as seen through the lens of an
artist and pinpointed by that ancient
city's young, space-age poets

THERE ARE AS MANY WAYS to observe London as there
are pigeons to make a shambles of Trafalgar Square. It is
timeless (ever stood in the Poets' Corner in Westminster
Abbey?), and it is of today (here are the miniest skirts!).
But it is London's day-by-dayness beneath the "kinky"
surface that preoccupies photographer Irving Penn. Tower
Bridge, above, a Harley Street surgeon's doorbell, right,
a mug of tea set on a step, next page, seem more basic
than the Beatles. To extend Penn's vision into words, LOOK
drew on the works of some of the young poets of England.
John Fairfax, whose anthology of verse *Listen to This*
(Longmans, Green & Co., Ltd.) is just out, says: "We try
to speak an international language. Some of us are influenced by the poet-scientist-priest Chardin. We are concerned with the space age and what is happening in
technical terms. We are thinkers as well as poets. We mix
classic with technological terms." His and other voices are
heard on the following pages.   PATRICIA COFFIN

PHOTOGRAPHED BY IRVING PENN

Regular features The many recurring pages and sections of a magazine play
an important role in determining format, but their particular place varies from
publication to publication. The contents page may occupy a minimum amount
of space if it is considered a minor service for conscientious readers, or it
may be assigned to an important promotional area; this depends on the nature
of the magazine and its editorial approach. The problem presented by the
contents is primarily typographic: because of the service aspect of this section,
it should be simple and readable. To preserve the unity of the format, all regular

121

Four of the most common size options for publications are shown in scale for comparison in the diagram at the right.

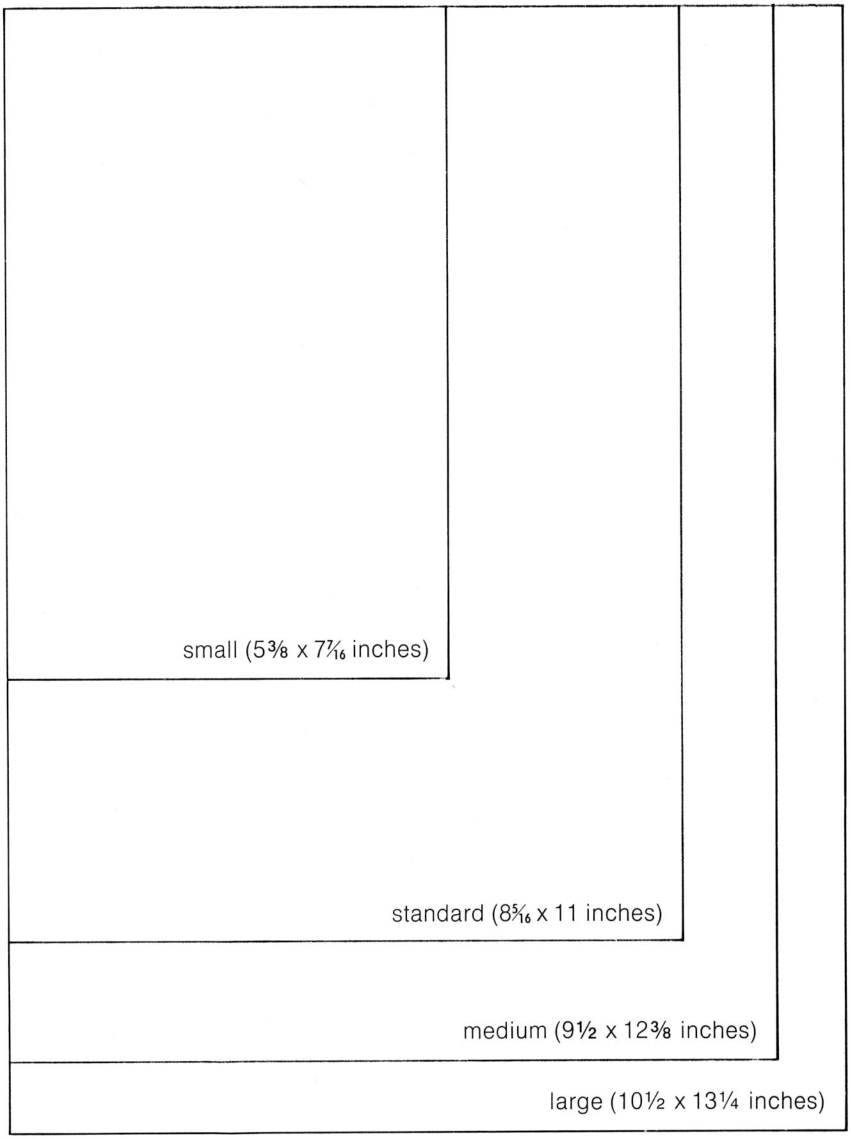

small (5⅜ x 7⅐ inches)

standard (8⁵⁄₁₆ x 11 inches)

medium (9½ x 12⅜ inches)

large (10½ x 13¼ inches)

features should be related to each other and to the balance of the magazine in typography and design.

Magazine production   The art director on today's mass magazines frequently is part of a quality-control group and becomes involved in decisions concerning the use of new production techniques and printing equipment.

While it is not essential that a publication designer be skilled in all of the techniques of printing production, it is valuable for him to know the limitations and, more important, the potential of the process with which he works. He will benefit by having a skilled production manager, and often achieve the best results when design and production planning are closely related.

It is not within the scope of this book to discuss reproduction processes in detail, but an outline of the three primary printing processes and their basic characteristics can serve as a guide to further study.

Letterpress   This is the earliest widely used process of printing, first used to print woodcuts. From it came Gutenberg's development of movable type. In letterpress printing, a raised printing surface comes in contact first with the ink and then with the paper.

Letterpress is practical for all types of magazines, but it is at its best when high-quality paper is available; the force of the impression tends to produce an uneven image on fibrous or rough paper.

Today, high-speed web presses and heat-set inks make letterpress extremely fast and therefore highly suitable for mass-circulation publications, but the process also has many advantages for smaller magazines. It has the potential for high quality, and it permits control in both printing and engraving. It is the only printing process that can print directly from type or type slugs, which is sometimes economical.

Lithography   Like the process used by the artist to produce lithographs, offset lithographic printing is based on the antipathy of oil and water. A line drawn with grease pencil on the surface of a polished stone will repel water applied to the surface. In turn, the water will repel the ink that is rolled across the stone, so when paper is pressed against it, only the image of the drawn line will be transferred to the paper.

In modern offset lithography, an etched zinc plate is ordinarily used in place of the stone, and the image is transferred (or offset) onto a rubber blanket, which in turn places the image on the paper.

Because offset lithography is not as fast as letterpress, it is rarely used for mass publication, but it is widely used by magazines with print runs of less than a million copies and is becoming standard for most business publications and house organs.

One strength of offset lithography is that its rubber blanket prints uniformly on all kinds of paper. Halftone reproduction in offset is also somewhat lower in cost than letterpress, but when costs are cut too fine, the halftones tend to be a flat, dull gray. Offset is also capable of producing excellent color when quality rather than cost is the primary consideration.

Gravure   This process is the opposite of letterpress in that the printing surface is incised into the printing plate rather than raised above it. After the plate is inked, it is scraped clean by a "doctor blade," and only the ink remaining in the depressions is transferred to the paper.

Sheet-fed gravure is the top quality form of this process. It is expensive and usually used only for fine books and expensive short-run magazines.

When rotogravure was first introduced into publication printing, it offered a high-speed method of reproducing halftones and color on paper of second-rate surface quality. It was particularly suitable for newspaper-supplement printing and mass magazines. Unfortunately, rotogravure failed to match the advances in speed and quality of the letterpress process during the period prior to and immediately following World War II, and use of the process declined.

The *Look-kromatic* process is a refinement of rotogravure that uses fast-drying inks and ultrafine screens and permits a concentration of color and resolution that makes it one of the finest current methods of large-scale publication printing.

The three basic printing processes discussed here are the only ones in general use. They all involve some form of direct contact between the printing plate or cylinder and the paper, and they all grew out of the Gutenberg revolution more than five hundred years ago. They are also out of step with the technological and scientific developments of the present day.

Today, many new methods of reproduction are in the research and development stage. Most of these bypass direct contact and transfer the image to the printed surface by ultrasonic, electrostatic, or photographic means. The rapid acceptance of any of these methods is blocked by the high cost of development, the time lag between prototype and the production line, the extensive inventory of unused existing equipment, and trade union attitudes. Finally, however, distribution problems will probably influence the determination of future production procedures more than mechanical ideas of press improvement.

Binding   There are three principal methods of holding the pages of a magazine together.

1. In saddle wire stitching, two or more staples are inserted through the fold and turned over in the center of the magazine. This is a relatively inexpensive binding, and magazines bound this way open flat. Saddle wire stitching has a few disadvantages. Because each page in the front half is continuous with a page in the back half, full-color pages in the front must match with pages in the back. If a special stock insert is used, it must appear in equal number of pages in both the front (low-folio) and back (high-folio). This binding also presents problems for publications with many pages: after trimming, the pages at the center become slightly narrower than those in the front and back. In production parlance this is called shingling. The designer must be aware of it when he designs the center pages, or he may find vital parts of the spreads bleeding off the edge of the page.

2. In side wire stitching, the magazine is folded into several booklet-like sections. These are held together by staples inserted near the binding edge of page one and turned over on the last page. The cover is then wrapped around the stapled magazine and pasted to the spine. This binding will accommodate many pages, and there is less risk of the cover or center spreads tearing away than with saddle wire stitching. In addition, inserts of special stock or special printing can be placed anywhere within the magazine. The disadvantage of the binding is its annoying habit of fighting the reader. The pages do not open flat, and they often act as though they wish they were closed. Also, the designer must be careful when he uses an image that extends across facing pages, because part of the picture will fold into the binding.

3. Perfect binding is a comparatively new method that until recently was practical only for publications with large production budgets and reasonably

small print orders. Perfect binding resembles the side-stitched binding in general form, but uses an adhesive instead of staples to hold the binding edge of the pages together. Perfect binding combines the virtues of both binding processes. Each spread opens fully flat, and the flexibility of makeup is superior even to that offered by side wire stitching. Perfect binding presents the designer with many creative opportunities. Special inserts of any number of pages, swatches, diecuts, gatefolds, and even phonograph records can be bound in to add variety to the visual presentation.

If perfect binding has a weakness, it is in the chemistry of its adhesives. Early versions of perfect binding tended to come apart when they were subjected to heat, but improved glue seems to have solved the problem.

The binding of magazines, like all technical aspects of publication production, is not truly up to date. Students of the magazine's future forecast many dramatic changes; among these are content electronically transmitted to computer-controlled printing centers; in-line printing machines that prepare the paper, print it, and bind it in one continuous operation; and even at-home printout of publications, with each issue tailored to the individual needs of each subscriber.

Whether any of these changes will take place, and when, and how are questions beyond the province of this book. But whatever its limitations today, publication design remains one of the most volatile and most exciting areas of contemporary communication.

Acknowledgments

It would have been impossible for me to write this book without the accumulated knowledge of the design profession. I am grateful to the many art directors, inside and outside of publishing, who have contributed to the mainstream of visual presentation, and hence to this book.

I am particularly indebted to my own staff at *Look* — to Leonard Jossel, Verne Noll, Charles Crandall, Joseph Tarallo, Philip Sykes, and William Hopkins, who served as my associate art directors; to William Townsend, William Rosivach, Jack Boydston, Al Ewers, and the many others who at one time or another have contributed to the excellence of *Look;* to Leemarie Burrows Bernstein, my assistant, who gave me invaluable help in the painstaking job of shaping and revising the text, illustrations, and credits.

It is impossible to enumerate all of the designers, artists, and photographers who have influenced the images reproduced here, or to adequately explain the omission of so much excellent work in visual presentation. The captions and the accompanying credits list the direct contributions wherever available information has made this possible.

The designer working in the contemporary publication field will encounter many problems that have not been dealt with in this book. The following bibliography points out some ways he can increase his understanding of the subject, but one of the most important sources for new directions in publication design cannot be listed. This is the magazines themselves. No recommendation can long survive the mercurial shifts in editorial attitudes or keep up with the frequent redeployment of publication designers.

The serious student of publication design should not limit his study to contemporary publications. Some of the comparatively old issues of magazines mentioned in Chapter 1 offer a surprising wealth of inspiration and, as yet, undeveloped ideas. The designer may serve his creative purpose even better by exploring sources outside of the publication field. By devoting himself to communication needs, new forms, and innovative techniques of presentation, he may be able to once again break the mold of publication design.

Bibliography

Color   Birren/Ostwald/Munsell. *Basic Color Library.* Van Nostrand Reinhold, 1970.
Jacobson, Egbert. *Basic Color.* Paul Theobald, 1948.

Design   The Art Directors Club. *Annual of Advertising and Editorial Art.* Watson-Guptill (1921-   ).
Banham, Reyner. *Theory and Design in the First Machine Age.* Rev. ed. Praeger, 1967.
Bauhaus. The Museum of Modern Art, 1938.
Gregory, R. L. *Eye and Brain: the psychology of seeing.* World University Library, 1966.
Herdeg, Walter (editor). *Graphis Annual.* Graphis Press (1952-   ).
Kepes, Gyorgy. *Language of Vision.* Paul Theobald, 1951.
Le Corbusier. *The Modulor.* Harvard University Press, 1954.
Rand, Paul. *Thoughts on Design.* 3rd ed. Van Nostrand Reinhold, 1971.
Tolmer, A. *Mise en Page.* Paris, 1930.
Wingler, Hans M. *The Bauhaus.* MIT Press, 1969.

Illustration   Fawcett, Robert. *On the Art of Drawing.* Watson-Guptill, 1958.
The Push Pin Style. Communications Arts Book, 1970.
The Society of Illustrators. *The Illustrators Annual.* Hastings House (1959-   ).

Photography   Herdeg, Walter (editor). *Photographis Annual.* Graphis Press (1951-   ).
Newhall, Beaumont. *The History of Photography.* The Museum of Modern Art, Doubleday, 1964.
Pollack, Peter. *The Picture History of Photography.* Harry N. Abrams, 1969.
Rothstein, Arthur. *Photojournalism.* Amphoto, 1965.

Typography   Burns, Aaron. Typography. Reinhold, 1961.
Hlavsa, Oldruich. *A Book of Type and Design.* Tudor, 1960.
Rosen, Ben. *Type and Typography.* Van Nostrand Reinhold, 1963.

Credits

All page layouts in this book, unless otherwise credited in the captions, were designed by Allen Hurlburt for *Look* magazine.
All photographs and illustrations, unless identified with other sources, are from *Look* and are copyrighted by Cowles Communications, Inc.

Photographs

11	Margaret Bourke-White
	Howard Sochurek
12	Richard Avedon
13	Herbert Matter
14	Ben Rose
15	Cal Bernstein
	Allan Arbus
16	Ralph Hattersley
25	Paul Fusco
29	Philip Harrington
30	Max Maxwell
31	Robert Freson
32	Bert Stern
33	Douglas Kirkland
34	Edward Steichen
35	Robert Freson
	Cornell Capa
	Eve Arnold
36	Frank Bauman
39	Apollo 8, NASA
42	Arthur Rothstein
43	Bob Adelman
44-47	Stanley Tretick
48	Ernst Haas

49	John Vachon
50-51	Art Kane
52	David Douglas Duncan
	Richard Avedon
53	James Karales
54	Art Kane
55	Philippe Halsman
	Marvin Newman
56	Neil Armstrong, Apollo 11, NASA
59	William Joli
	Seymour Mednick
68	Richard Avedon
69	Arnold Newman
70	Richard Avedon
73	Douglas Kirkland
74-75	Irving Penn
76	Marvin Newman
77	Fred Maroon
	Stanley Tretick
	Douglas Jones
	Dan McCoy
	UPI
78	Various
79	Marc Riboud
	Apollo 11, NASA
85	Arthur Rothstein
88	Joel Baldwin
99	Paul Fusco
100	Dennis Stock
109	Dennis Stock
114	Pete Turner
	Arnold Newman
	Paul Fusco

Various
115 Bert Stern
    Thomas Weir
    Bill King
    Alberto Rizzo
116 Steve Phillips
    Phil Narco
    Bill Cadge
117 Will McBride
    Pete Turner
    Various
118 Bill Buerge
119 Dick Hess
    Donald McCullin
121 Irving Penn

    Art and Illustration
  8 M. F. Agha
    Covarrubias
 10 T. M. Clelland
    Paul Rand
 12 Alexey Brodovitch
 15 Henry Wolf
 16 Richard Lindner
 17 Seymour Chwast
 24 Poliphilus, Pierpont Morgan Library
 26 Mondrian, The Museum of
    Modern Art

 27 Le Corbusier, from the Modular
 40 Josef Albers
 58 Ben Shahn
 59 Paul Davis
    Jack Gregory
 60 Robert Fawcett
 61 Austin Briggs
62-63 Norman Rockwell
 64 David Levine
    Andre François
 65 Milton Glaser
    George Giusti
    Rembrandt Peale, N.Y. Historical
    Society
 66 Bernie Fuchs
 72 Saul Steinberg
 94 Detail, Bible, Mainz, Johann
    Gutenberg, 1454-55.
    Detail, Nicolas Jenson, Venice,
    1471, Pierpont Morgan Library.
110 Gabriel Czakany
113 Picasso, The Museum of Modern
    Art, New York
115 Milton Glaser
    Special diagrams and charts for
    this book were prepared by Jack
    Taromina and Al Ewers.

Index

A

Advertising and form, 67-68, 73
    typography, 108
Agha, M. F., 8, 9, 11, 98
Albers, Josef, 40
American Magazine, The, 14
Ameryka, 114
Ansel, Ruth, 115
Apparel Arts, 10
Artwork and graphics, 57-66
    applications, 59, 61-62
Asymmetry, 25, 28
Avant Garde, 16, 101, 115
Avedon, Richard, 70

B

Back Packer, 21
Balance, 28, 30
Baskerville (typeface), 102
Beall, Lester, 10
Bernard, Walter, 18
Binding, 125-126
Bleed, 8, 9, 23
    type, 99
Bodoni, Giambattista, 96
Bodoni (typeface), 102, 105
Book design, 23, 24
Briggs, Austin, 57
Brodovitch, Alexey, 8-9, 11, 13
Burtin, Will, 11

C

Cadge, William, 116
Campbell, Heyworth, 7

Caption typography, 106, 108-109
Century Expanded (typeface), 102
Chermayeff, Ivan, 117
Clelland, T. M., 7, 9
Cold-type composition, 92-95
    and display typography, 106-107
Colliers, 14
Color, 83-86
    harmony, 82
    notation, 82
    proofs, 86
    reproduction, 86
    theory, 83
Computer composition, 92, 93, 94
Contrast, 32-33, 34-37
    chromatic, 84
    value, 32, 36
    volume, 32, 36
Copyfitting, 104
Continuous format, 68
Corbusier, Le, 26-27, 28, 90
Covers, 68, 100, 120
Crowninshield, Frank, 7

D

Davis, Paul, 59
De Stijl, 25- 26, 86
Didot, Firmin, 96, 100
    typeface, 105
Display typography, 106-107, 110
Domus, 18
Dreyfus, Henry, 9
Dwiggins, W. A., 7

E

Editorial concept
  and art direction, 8, 13-14, 23
Em, 100-101
Emergency Medicine, 119
En, 100-101
Eros, 16
Esquire, 15, 18

F

Fact, 17
Fawcett Robert, 57, 60
Feitler, Bea, 115,
Fiction illustration, 57, 59
Fleckhaus, Willy, 16, 22, 117
Folio, 21, 116
Format and style, 67-80
  and advertising, 67-68
  and reading patterns, 73, 76
Fortune, 7, 10
François, Andre, 64
Fuchs, Bernie, 66
Futura (typeface), 105

G

Gestalt psychology, 37-38
Giusti, George, 65
Glaser, Milton, 21, 65
Gothic typefaces, 98
Gravure, 124
Gregory, Jack, 59
Grid system, 27, 87-90
Griffo, Francesco, 23, 96
Grotesque typefaces, 98
Gutenberg, Johann, 23, 94

H

Haas, Ernst, 48
Halsman, Philippe, 55
Harper's Bazaar, 15, 115
Helk, Peter, 57
Helvetica (typeface), 102-104
Hopkins, Will, 88, 114
Hot-type composition, 92-93
  and display typography, 106

Humor illustration, 59, 64

I

Illusion(s), 37-40
Illustration, artwork and
  graphics, 57-66
  applications, 59, 61-62
  history, 60, 61
Illustration, photographic, 41-56, 57, 58
  categories, 41, 43, 44
  picture selection, 53-55

J

Jenson, Nicolas, 94, 96

K

Kane, Art, 14, 50, 54

L

La Gatta, John, 57
Layout, 111-123
  comprehensive, 111
  covers, 120
  fitting pictures, 112
  grid system, 87-90
  regular features, 121-123
  rough, 111
Lettering
  hand and photo-, 107, 110
Letterpress, 123
Levine, David, 64
Leyendecker, J. C., 57
Liberman, Alexander, 11
Lichtenstein, Roy, 57
Life, 11, 118
Linotype, 92, 93
Lithography, 123-124
Lois, George, 18
London Times, 20, 119
Look, 4, 9, 15, 18, 113
Look-kromatic process, 124
Lubalin, Herb, 14, 16, 101, 115
Luce, Henry, 9
Lustig, Alvin, 14

M

McCall's, 13-14, 15
Manutius, Aldus, 23
Mineral Digest, 119
Modern typefaces, 96
Mondrian, Piet, 25- 26
Moore, Dave, 117
Morgan, Wallace, 57
Ms., 21
Muller-Brockman, Josef, 90
Müller-Lyer illusion, 37-38

N

Newman, Arnold, 69
Newman, Marvin, 55
New York, 19, 21
Noll, Verne, 48
Notan, 32
   see also Value relationship
Nova, 21, 118

O

Old style typefaces, 96, 106
Optical illusions, 37-40
Ostwald, Wilhelm, 82

P

Page design
   development, 7- 22
   elements, 23-40
Parker, Al, 57
Parrish, Maxfield, 57
Paul, Arthur, 13, 19
Peck, Priscilla, 11
Penn, Irving, 74, 121
Perception, 37-40
   see also Illusion(s)
Perfect binding, 125-126
Photograph(s)
   cropping, 33, 112
   evaluation, 85
   fitting to layout, 112
   selection, 54, 55
Photographic illustration; see Illustration,
   photographic

Photography
   influence of, 9, 41
   technique, 51, 53
Photojournalism, 9, 41, 43
Pica, 100
Picture essay, 44, 48
Picture story, 43-44
Pineles, Cipe, 11
Playboy, 13, 19
Point, 100
Poliphilus, 23, 24
Portfolio, 11-13
Production, 123-126
   binding, 125-126
   gravure, 124
   letterpress, 123
   lithography, 123, 124
Psychology Today, 19, 118
Push Pin Studio, 57

Q

Queen, 21

R

Rand, Paul, 10, 30
Rauschenberg, Robert, 57
Reading patterns
   and format, 73, 76
Redbook, 116
Regular features
   layout, 121-123
Renner, Paul, 105
Reproduction
   color, 84-86
   see also Production
Rockwell, Norman, 57, 66-63
Rolling Stone, 17
Rose, Ben, 14

S

Saddle wire stitching, 125
Sans-serif typefaces, 96, 98
Saturday Evening Post, 14, 17
Science illustration, 61

Seventeen, 14
Shahn, Ben, 58
Side wire stitching, 125
Space, 24-31
Steichen, Edward, 34
Steinberg, Saul, 72
Stern, Bert, 32
Storch, Otto, 13, 15
Structural typefaces, 96, 98
Sykes, Philip, 52
Symmetry, 26-27

T
Tarallo, Joe, 49
Tatami mats, 25
Television
   effect of, 17
Text typography, 102-104, 107-108
Thompson, Bradbury, 10, 11
Times Roman (typeface), 102
Transitional typefaces, 96
Tretick, Stanley, 44
Tudor, Charles, 9-10, 11
Twen, 16, 117
Typefaces
   anatomy of, 95, 97
   classifications, 96, 98-99
   color, 95, 101
   dominant text, 102-104
   examples, 94, 96, 97, 104 -108
   legibility of, 95, 102

   measurement, 100-102
Typography, 91-110
   caption, 106
   display, 106-107
   processes, 92-95
   regular features, 121
   standards for captions, 108-109
   standards for display, 110
   standards for text, 107-108

V
Vachon, John, 49
Value relationship, 32-34
Van Doesburg, Theo, 26
Vanity Fair, 8
Vignelli, Massimo, 90
Von Schmidt, Harold, 57

W
Warhol, Andy, 57
Widow, 108
Wolf, Henry, 13, 15
Woman's Home Companion, 14
Wyeth, N.C., 57

X
X height, 97, 101-102

Z
Zachary, Frank, 11, 13
Zoom, 20

Designed by Allen Hurlburt
Type set by Cooper & Beatty, Limited, Toronto
Printed and bound by Halliday Lithograph Corporation